THE BRYANT FAMILY VINEYARD COOKBOOK

THE
Bryant Family Vineyard
COOKBOOK

RECIPES FROM GREAT CHEFS AND FRIENDS

BARBARA BRYANT WITH BETSY FENTRESS

PHOTOGRAPHY BY ROBERT HOLMES

Andrews McMeel
Publishing, LLC
Kansas City

09 10 11 12 13 SDB 10 9 8 7 6 5 4 3 2 1

Library of Congress Cataloging-in-Publication Data

Bryant, Barbara.
    The Bryant Family Vineyard cookbook : recipes from great chefs and friends / Barbara Bryant with Betsy Fentress ; photography by Robert Holmes. — 1st ed.
        p. cm.
        Includes index.
        ISBN-13: 978-0-7407-6977-1
        ISBN-10: 0-7407-6977-4
    1. Cookery. 2. Wine and wine making. 3. Bryant family. 4. Bryant Family Vineyard. I. Fentress, Betsy. II. Bryant Family Vineyard. III. Title.

    TX714.B796 2008
    641.5—dc22
                                2008002365

Design by Holly Camerlinck
Letterpress recipe titles printed by The Craftboy Workshop in Kansas City, Missouri

www.andrewsmcmeel.com

Recipes printed with the permission of:
Michael Anthony, Daphne Araujo, Dan Barber, Lidia Bastianich, Christopher Bennett, Vince P. Bommarito, Daniel Boulud, Bertrand Bouquin, Terrance Brennan, Scott Bryan, Barbara Bryant, Bill Cardwell, Bryan Carr, Narsai David, Bernard Dervieux, James Fiala, Larry Forgione, Josh Galliano, Gale Gand, Alexandra Guarnaschelli, Thomas Keller, Sirio Maccioni, Christopher Manning, Matthew McGuire, Kevin Nashan, Cindy Pawlcyn, Richard Perry, Nora Pouillon, Richard Reddington, Julie Ridlon, Eric Ripert, Lou Rook III, Michael Rozzi, Pilar Sanchez, Celina Tio, Rick Tramonto, Charlie Trotter, Jean-Georges Vongerichten, David Waltuck, Patricia Wells, Aaron Wright

The Artichoke and Radicchio Clafouti recipe on page 2, the Mediterranean Tomato-Lemon Tart recipe on page 16, the Roasted Turkey Breast recipe on page 104, and the Chocolate Mousse recipe on page 136 were adapted with permission from *Daniel's Dish: Entertaining at Home with a Four-Star Chef* by Daniel Boulud, Filipacchi Publishing, 2003.

The Braised Cardamom Beef Stew recipe on page 90 was adapted with permission from *Charlie Trotter Cooks at Home* by Charlie Trotter, Ten Speed Press, 2000.

Photos by Barbara M. Bryant: pages x, xiv, xix, xxii, xxiii

In thanksgiving for our parents, around whose tables we first broke bread, and who always had room for one more.

Contents

Acknowledgments

There are so many people to thank for their encouragement and help with this project. From the very start Ed Morgan and Emily Solway and their team at the Bowery Mission in New York gave their time to talk about how we could use this book to help others. The Mission serves those who, though caught in cycles of poverty, hopelessness, and dependencies, have made the first step in turning their lives around by showing up at its doorstep. Through its programs, the Bowery Mission supports those who want to reclaim their lives and begin afresh; that is the vision that inspired us to write this book. A portion of the proceeds from the sales will go to the Mission.

To our chef friends from all over the country who so eagerly contributed recipes and supported the project, we express our heartfelt gratitude. Most had deadlines and pressures of their own, but they always responded with cheer and professionalism—there would be no book without them.

To all those who love Bryant Family Vineyard Cabernet, who appreciate its uniqueness, who want to share it, and who are curious about the place from which it comes—you have helped make this wine beloved throughout the world.

To Bob Holmes—your extraordinary photographs are a gift to all. You have truly captured the little piece of heaven on earth that is Bryant Family Vineyard.

To our publisher, Kirsty Melville, editors Jean Lucas and Lane Butler, and the entire team at Andrews McMeel, thank you for your enthusiasm and belief in this project. Harriet Bell, to our great delight, provided invaluable editorial direction and encouragement at crucial times.

To Betsy Fentress, my business partner and friend "extraordinaire," for her energy, organization, and gifts of laughter and time, and to her beautiful family who have included me in the most wonderful dinner parties—the best kind of gatherings—full of warmth, laughter, conversation, and people of all ages enjoying each other, fabulous food, and the wines we all brought to share.

To Charlie Trotter, Park Smith, Jimmy Fiala, Janice Fuhrman, Anna Monticelli, and Patricia Wamhoff, for sharing their expertise in making and enjoying wine and food, pairing the two, and giving their time to write about it.

To Denise Landis, our energetic recipe tester, who graciously dealt with many changes while sharing her love of good food.

For guiding us with their knowledge of publishing and providing helpful introductions, we thank Daniel Boulud, Morgan Entrekin, Dan Halpern, Stephen Koenig, Tamara Traeder, and especially our agent, Lisa Queen.

To dear friends and family in St. Louis, California, Washington, Naples, New York, London, and Rwanda whose support during the years helped bring this project to fruition. A special thanks to Ken Harrington and the Hatchery Team at the Washington University MBA Program.

Mary Ann Steiner, Susie Barron, Christina Bryant, and Linda Williams provided invaluable help with manuscript preparation and technical support. Rebecca Waltman and Kevin Kerwin have been instrumental in expanding our culinary world beyond measure; their gifts are extraordinary.

We are grateful to our friends in California and throughout the country who introduced us to chefs and food and wine writers—Vic Motto, Peb Jackson, Polly Pollack, Annie Presley Selanders, and the Naples Winter Wine Festival Board.

To Don Bryant, for all your work in developing Bryant Family Vineyard. To Caroline and Dan Wojtkowiak, Mark Aubert, John Piña and his team, who planted, pruned and harvested—thank you for your year-round efforts and devotion to the winemaking process. We celebrate the fruits of your diligent work.

To my children—Derek, Christina, and Justin—you are God's very best gifts to me, reminding me that in no way is 60 too old to start a new career.

BARBARA BRYANT

x

This project, five years in the making, was inspired and driven by Barbara Bryant. We met briefly nearly 25 years before she began her idea for sharing the gifts of her vineyard with the less fortunate, and upon our chance reuniting, discovered within the space of a few hours that we were eager to collaborate on this book. She brings so much to this project—not only the Bryant Family Cabernet Sauvignon, magnanimous chef friends, and kitchen know-how, but most especially her indefatigable spirit—all centered around her love of family and friends and serving them at the table. Her arms gather a much larger crowd, though, through her devotion to the life-changing work at the Bowery Mission. The homeless, hungry, and downtrodden men and women who finally find themselves, by grace I like to think, at the Mission can take comfort in knowing they are part of what she considers her extended family. I am happy to share her vision of just how big her "table" can be.

Special thanks to my Connell brothers and sisters spread across the country, who have always been there to make lively, fun-filled holidays and celebrations go on endlessly. I hope, no matter where we all gather, that the celebrating continues. And to the Nashville Fentresses, I am indebted to your warm and loving Southern hospitality.

I am most grateful to my husband, Sam, for loving the spirit of a large family and embracing it, and for his endless patience and cheer during the many phases of this book. Our children, Madeleine, Clare, Jane, Paul, Sam, and Joseph, are my joy and inspiration in and out of the kitchen; through them I have learned so much about the importance of sharing our day over a meal, and that sometimes, it is not a stretch to say that food does equal love.

BETSY FENTRESS

Foreword

BY PARK B. SMITH

I am a very privileged and fortunate man. Privileged because I count Barbara Bryant as a dear friend, and fortunate because I have had the opportunity to experience the food of many of the chefs who contributed to this cookbook.

Barbara is one of those rare and fine individuals so difficult to describe. She is gifted and accomplished in the kitchen. She has been a passionate vintner, a gracious hostess, and, most importantly, a loving and giving person.

All of the chefs who contributed to this book are true artists. Their culinary delights are best appreciated when teamed with an equally artistic winemaker. Food and wine are natural complements to one another. There is so much that can be said about the pairing of wine and food, and Barbara has asked both chefs and a sommelier to provide insightful and knowledgeable suggestions for the appropriate wines to accompany the recipes in this book.

I firmly believe that if the winemaker and chef have done their jobs well, then any wine you love can be enjoyed with any food you desire.

Given that the recipes in this book are by some of the finest chefs in the world, they should be complemented by some of the finest wines. If you go to the effort of making a memorable meal, you should then make the effort to choose a wine worthy to be served with it. Barbara has made that task simpler by including wine pairings.

To prepare a fine meal and enjoy it with a good wine is a treat; to do so with family and friends is an act of love. Given this, it is not surprising that a portion of the profits from this book will benefit New York's Bowery Mission and that all the chefs Barbara contacted readily donated their time and recipes. It is now time for you to share your passion for food and wine. Invite your friends. Select the best ingredients you can find. Take the time to prepare everything with care. Create a memorable setting. Choose the appropriate wines. Then indulge yourself in two of life's greatest pleasures—food and wine. *Bon appétit.*

Introduction

BY CHARLIE TROTTER

The Bryant Family Vineyard is located in one of the most magnificent settings in the Napa Valley. The winery basks in glowing sunshine and is abundant with beautiful fruit. High above the Valley, on Pritchard Hill, the Vineyard literally radiates the warmth of the Bryants individually and as a family. They have always understood the meaning of hospitality through sharing their table with others. They also recognize how welcoming cuisine can be when prepared with the freshest and most pristine of ingredients, and they value the experience of pairing such food with fine wine.

Since 1992, the grapes grown in the stony soil along Lake Hennessey in Napa Valley have resulted in the gorgeous Cabernet Sauvignons from the Bryant Family Vineyard. The wines have rightfully won international recognition. Customers have appreciated these extraordinary wines in our restaurant for many years. The wines are elegantly styled, with luscious black fruit and velvety tannins; they are the culmination of years of hard work and love of the earth, along with a deep appreciation of vines. This same level of thoughtfulness is demonstrated in *The Bryant Family Vineyard Cookbook*.

Throughout the years, the Bryant Family wines have been enjoyed by oenophiles around the world. These enthusiasts have gathered at tables with friends and family, partaken of an exquisite bottle of Bryant Family Cabernet Sauvignon, and feasted on some of the delectable dishes you will find in this book. Many of us have added recipes to honor the great labor and success of the Bryant Family Vineyard. The noble art of making wine is synergized with the scrumptious food in this cookbook. In fact, I just might use this book in our kitchen and not bother to create more dishes, as the finest ones are already right here.

I raise my glass to the Bryants and to all the people who work and care for the fruit at the Bryant Family Vineyard.

The Story

BY BARBARA BRYANT WITH JANICE FUHRMAN

Trying to capture in words the unique beauty of the land that is now Bryant Family Vineyard is both humbling and daunting. I remember in such a fresh way my first experience of that very special place. I can still feel the chill in the air—dry, cold but refreshing rather than penetrating. The quiet was proverbially audible with soft rustlings of leaves and bird songs punctuating it in high definition. Although I had never been there, it felt like home. It was mid-spring: There were wild iris and lupine vibrantly purple on the green hills and huge swaths of yellow mustard flower on the valley floor. The morning fog was blanketing Lake Hennessey and the view of St. Helena in the distance. In the daylight the fog quickly burned off and the lake sparkled; as night fell the sparkling shifted to the lights of the town.

I had just returned from the beautiful Burgundy region of France and was enjoying the contrast of landscapes: Napa's steeper hills to their gentler ones and the younger, straighter Napa vines to Burgundy's ancient gnarled ones. I was also enjoying all that the Burgundian vintners and the California vintners share, particularly the attentive cultivation of land that yields wonderful grapes. Both have such joy and pride in making wine and sharing it with others.

There are so many scenes of the vineyard that I love—the view when sitting between the rows of vines while looking down toward the lake, the way that vista constantly changes depending on the time of day and season, the shapes of the leaves, the clusters of dusty, blue mature grapes, and dried prunings on the dry earth. Even on cold, rainy, late-winter days and blistering hot summer afternoons, it is a place to pause, look, and look again, delight in, and be thankful for. It is a place to stand in one spot and slowly turn a full 360 degrees.

Picnic lunches at the vineyard have always been magical. If the weather is too cool, or rainy, or extra warm, lunch in the winery dining room offers a view of the vineyard hill dramatically sloping toward serene Lake Hennessey, where Canada geese, bald eagles, and ospreys seek sanctuary. Homemade wheat bread, French baguettes, pâtés, sausages, cheeses and cornichons complement the Bryant Family Cabernet perfectly.

Sage Canyon Road is a private drive, and thus the vineyard and winery cannot be open to the public. The very few events we have hosted there have been memorable. In the early days, when there was no building on the property, we set up tables on the crest of the hill under the lone live oak overlooking the vines and the shimmering lake. The tables had crisp white linens, beautiful loaves of bread, sheaves of wheat, and jars of flowers. Besides the idyllic weather, the air was filled with the anticipation of soon being able to taste the wine that our guests from across the country had traveled so far to experience. I can still see the sun low on the horizon, backlighting the wine in the glasses—that rich, deep cabernet color. I can still recall the joy of the tasters. It was an event that lingers in my memory. In my mind, it encapsulates the best of the wine world, whether it is in a small trattoria in Tuscany sharing an unknown harvest, in a musty cellar in Burgundy, or on a sloping Napa hillside: friends enjoying life and its good gifts of camaraderie, conversation, nature, food, and wine.

We've also shared wonderful times in the cellar. Softly lit, the library of bottles casts a wonderful glow on the area where the tables are usually set. The acoustics are perfect for live music, and local caterers do a fantastic job.

In the early years, before the winery was built, the wine was made and bottled at a co-op in Oakville that caters to boutique vineyards. It was a great event for me to go there and taste from the barrels. The setting was not glamorous, but I adored the simplicity of it and the yeasty smell. We always had Riedel glasses, a jar of fresh flowers, and a crusty baguette. The air was chilly and thick with the fragrance of the oak barrels and of grapes turning into wine.

Wine has a personal role in many of life's events; there is something intimate about sharing food and wine. It helps to soften the edges of the day. It produces a climate in which friendships and relationships begin and are nurtured, events are celebrated, ideas germinated and developed. It elevates the ordinary, bringing celebration to family, marriages, and friendships as we put work aside and plan time to be together and share conversation, a meal, and a toast.

In the winter, when the Napa Valley floor is bright with the swaying gold of wild mustard, the fourteen acres of Cabernet Sauvignon vines are bare, brown, and woody, settling down in the muddy fields for a much-needed rest from the year before. This period of hibernation is deceiving. Like the seasons of life, when it seems as if nothing is happening but later you realize that so much has changed, so it is in the vineyards. The vines are preserving their life-giving force, biding their time until warmer weather and longer days arrive.

Harvest equipment has been put away until the next season, and barrels full of wine are developing in the 8,000-square-foot cave burrowed into the mountainside. But this is not a restful time for those who work in the vineyards, who are busy pruning the vineyards to control vine growth for the following season. They take up their shears in the cold and gloom of winter to cut back dead wood and plant growth, directing the plants' energies to develop flavor in the berries rather than vigorous vine growth.

In early spring, at bud-break, small, tender shoots emerge, and then clusters of grapes, classified as berries because they grow on vines, start to form. The vines are doing their job—drinking in the water and nutrients from the soil. The hills surrounding the vineyard are carpeted in emerald, and sunlight washes over the rock walls rimming the property. Chirping birds provide the background music for vineyard workers who are busily managing vine canopies, weeding, spraying, and otherwise encouraging nature along. Picturesque Lake Hennessey glistens below, protecting the steep hillside vineyards against frost. In the winery, we might be bottling an earlier vintage, and our winemakers are tasting wines from the different vineyard blocks and deciding how to blend them together.

In late July and early August, *véraison* occurs. This is the stage of the growing season when hard green grapes soften and redden on the vines. The land has grown drier, pruned leaves and stems lay about on the sun-baked earth, and the surrounding unplanted hills are now golden. The vineyard has filled out and is an undulating sea of bright greenery hugging the bulge of the hills. By late summer, the cabernet vines

are alive with vibrant color and swelling berries ripening with sugars. During the hot days of summer and early fall, the lake serves to help keep the vineyard cool as winds gust over it before blowing through our vineyard. The growing anticipation for that year's harvest is always leavened by the worry that nature might not cooperate this year and deliver us the conditions necessary for the finest of wine grapes. Like all farmers everywhere, winemakers are constantly aware that perfection in nature is seldom a sure thing and can never be taken for granted.

By fall, the vines are bursting with fruit and ready to be made into wine. The winery, too, is full of life and activity, as the winemakers taste from the various vineyard blocks to determine their moment of perfect ripeness. Determining when to pick the grapes is one of the most significant decisions in the entire winemaking process. For the Bryant Family Cabernet Sauvignon, which is a bold California wine, we want the grapes to have the perfect sugar levels and mature seeds that contribute to making a great wine.

Harvest is a joyful time at Bryant Family Vineyard. I wish I could share the feel of the grapes at sorting. Picked when it is very early—before dawn—they are very cool to the touch. And the colors are amazing, with skins so blue, juice so milky-dusty pink. The sound of them going into the tanks—the sound of rain, of raining grapes—is delightfully familiar and comforting. Harvest mornings are always full of anticipation and quiet scurrying. Once again, a group of loyal grape pickers has gathered together to collect the bounty of the long season's work. Doughnuts and coffee are picked up for everyone at a bakery in town, and there are smiles and greetings between people of different languages, all bundled up against the early chill. Nearby, trays are piled high to fill with grapes, and tractors are ready to haul them up to the winery as the sun climbs in the sky, almost above the horizon of Pritchard Hill. The fog begins to melt, and a peaceful silence reigns as hawks soar overhead. There has been great joy in learning more about winemaking and all that brings the grapes from "vine to wine."

In the winery, the plump grapes are hand-sorted twice. As we sift through the piles we

purge the mixture of leaves, tiny insects, "raisins," and mashed berries—anything we do not want in our final blend. The fruit is then delivered to a machine that gently separates the grapes from their stems, leaving the berries whole, not crushed, and they are left to sit in cold tanks for a few days.

Now the magic begins. Fermentation (when yeasts react with the grapes to convert their sugars into alcohol) takes place in the ten fermenters, custom-designed for us to develop separately the ten different vineyard blocks we have. We use the natural yeasts that live on the grape skins and that are naturally present in the environment in this process. After fermentation, the juice will steep further with the grape skins and the seeds; the whole process will take about three to four weeks. This soaking helps to transfer important characteristics to the finished wine, making it deeper and darker in color and with more concentrated flavor.

Next, the juice from the grapes goes into new French oak barrels to age for anywhere from eighteen months to two years. The new barrels mean that the oak will play an important role in the final wine. Just as high-quality grapes are a key ingredient in making fine wine, so are prime oak barrels a critical component. The oak imparts flavor and allows other characteristics, such as texture, to develop. The barrels can also soften the wine and enrich flavors and aromas.

These fine French barrels shelter the new wine in the cavernous space we had built into a hillside that abuts the winery. The cave neither takes up treasured open space nor requires energy use. It keeps the wines at ideal temperatures and humidity levels as they mature. Caves like ours are found throughout Napa Valley because they provide the ideal location for aging wine.

The vines in each of the ten vineyard blocks face different directions. Some are steeper than others, which results in each block receiving a different amount of sun exposure during the growing season. This also means they produce juices with different characteristics. Most or all of these blocks will be represented in the final blend that we will bottle as Bryant Family Vineyard Cabernet Sauvignon. The winemaker's challenge is to take the best and most interesting characteristics of each of these lots and blend them together into a seamless whole.

Once the wine is removed from the barrels, leaving the dead yeasts and other sediment behind, it is bottled and then aged for another year in the caves. It takes nearly three years and the effort and energy of twenty-five people to produce just 1,000 bottles of each vintage of a Bryant Family Vineyard

wine. Like many of God's gifts, the process that takes the raw material to the perfected product requires creativity, vision, hard work, and time.

As the days get shorter with the approaching winter season, the leaves on the vines turn yellow and fall to the ground, and once again the vines are bare—a bittersweet time for the Napa Valley vintners, but for the knowledge that this wondrous cycle will soon begin again.

Bryant Family Vineyard has been a wonderful gift. Finding the vineyard on Pritchard Hill, planting new vines, and waiting for them to mature was the beginning of the story. The grapes that grow there found exactly the right soil, sunlight, wind, and water. A combination of old winemaking traditions and new technologies have allowed the Bryant Family cabernet to age into a classic wine. That it became such a wonderful wine has allowed me the privilege of sharing it with others who then make their own memories—these are the best parts of the story.

This book is an intimate celebration of a place, a wine, and the people who cherish and share it. Not merely an anthology of great recipes, it is a celebration to which each guest chef has brought a favorite dish that none of us will forget. We pass these gifts on to you.

ON THE WINE PAIRINGS

We chose not to make this a cabernet cookbook or to limit the chefs to recipes that could be paired with Bryant Family Vineyard Cabernet Sauvignon. Instead we asked each chef to contribute his or her signature dishes—some of which do match perfectly with a California Cabernet.

Much has been written about wine pairing. In most cookbooks, specific wines are matched with each dish. On paper, the match may be exquisite, but cooks may not have the wine in their cellars, or may not be able to find it in a local wine shop. We think it is better to suggest a wine style for each recipe, which is what we have done in these pages. After planning the menu, each cook can then go to the cellar or wine shop and find the wines suggested—or even invite a wine consultant to recommend a comparable wine. Our suggestions are just that—suggestions. It is important to experiment and discover for yourself what pleases your own palate.

Barbara Bryant and Jim Fiala

First Courses

Artichoke and Radicchio Clafouti

DANIEL BOULUD

A clafouti is traditionally a pudding-like dessert from the Limousin region of France made with cherries or other stone fruit. When Daniel Boulud puts a savory spin on this classic, he includes my favorite spring vegetables—baby artichokes and radicchio. Vegetables are cooked, then arranged in a shallow baking dish, topped with a yeasty batter, and baked.

SERVES 6

2 large eggs, at room temperature

3 large egg whites, at room temperature

4 teaspoons sugar

½ cup heavy cream

1 teaspoon firmly packed fresh cake yeast

¼ cup all-purpose flour

7 tablespoons extra virgin olive oil

6 tablespoons freshly squeezed lemon juice

2 cups water

20 small baby artichokes

Nonstick cooking spray, for pan

2 ounces pancetta or bacon, cut into ¼-inch dice (optional)

Salt and freshly ground black pepper

8 white mushrooms, sliced ¼ inch thick

1 large shallot, finely diced

2 ounces arugula

1 small head radicchio (about ¾ pound), leaves separated

PREPARE THE BATTER: In a medium bowl, whisk together the eggs, egg whites, and sugar; set aside. In a small saucepan, gently heat the heavy cream until it is barely warm. Remove from the heat and add the yeast, stirring until smooth. Stir the cream into the egg mixture and whisk in the flour, followed by 2 tablespoons of the olive oil. Cover with plastic wrap and refrigerate for 1 hour.

Combine 3 tablespoons of the lemon juice and 2 cups water in a large bowl. Trim the artichoke stems and snap off the outer leaves until the remaining leaves are half yellow and half green. Cut off and discard the green tips. Slice the artichokes in half lengthwise and drop them into the lemon water.

Preheat the oven to 300°F. Spray a 6 by 2-inch round cake pan with nonstick cooking spray. Put the cake pan on a baking sheet.

Heat 1 tablespoon of the olive oil in a medium skillet over high heat. When the pan is hot but not smoking, add the pancetta and cook, stirring frequently, for 1 minute. Drain the artichokes and pat them dry. Add them to the pan along with 1½ tablespoons of the remaining lemon juice. Decrease the heat to medium and season with salt and pepper to taste. Cover and cook, stirring occasionally, until the artichokes are tender, 10 to 12 minutes. Transfer to a plate.

Add 1 tablespoon of the olive oil to the same pan. Add the mushrooms and shallot, then season with salt and pepper to taste. Sauté for 3 minutes, add the arugula and one-quarter of the radicchio, and season with salt and pepper. Sauté until the arugula and radicchio have just wilted, about 2 minutes. Line a plate with paper towels and transfer the vegetables to the plate to cool. Chop coarsely and set aside.

COOK THE CLAFOUTI: Remove the clafouti batter from the refrigerator. Stir the mushroom mixture into the clafouti batter. Season with salt and pepper. Pour half of the batter into the prepared pan and sprinkle the artichoke-pancetta mixture on top. Cover with the remaining batter (the pan should be about three-quarters full). Bake for 35 to 40 minutes, until a knife inserted in the middle comes out clean.

Tear the remaining radicchio leaves into large pieces and place in a bowl. Whisk together the remaining 1½ tablespoons lemon juice and remaining 3 tablespoons olive oil. Toss the dressing with the radicchio and season with salt and pepper to taste. Unmold the clafouti, re-invert right side up, and cut into 6 wedges. Divide the radicchio among 6 plates and add a slice of hot clafouti to each.

Wine pairing Artichokes pose a wine-pairing dilemma because they contain cynarin, a natural substance that makes most wines taste either sweet or bitter and metallic when paired with artichokes. Try white wines with crisp acidity and citrusy characteristics, such as a Verdicchio from the Marches region of Italy or a Grüner Veltliner from Austria.

Layered Beet and Goat Cheese Salad with Greens and Sherry Vinaigrette

JAMES FIALA

Alternating layers of roasted beets and goat cheese combined with mascarpone and pine nuts make this a colorful starter when served with salad greens. This is a beautiful salad with an architectural look achieved by using a ring mold, available in good cooking shops and online (you'll need four). Or you can do what Jimmy and many chefs do—go to the hardware store and have PVC pipe cut to just the right size! I often serve this as a first course at dinner parties.

SERVES 4

SHERRY VINAIGRETTE

1 shallot, finely diced

2 tablespoons sherry vinegar

1 cup extra virgin olive oil

Salt and cracked (lightly crushed)
     black peppercorns

4 large gold or red beets, with 2 to 3 inches
     stem attached

Salt

1 cup crumbled fresh goat cheese

½ cup (¼ pound) mascarpone cheese

3 tablespoons toasted pine nuts

½ cup coarsely chopped Italian parsley

3 shallots, finely diced

2 teaspoons extra virgin olive oil

Freshly ground black pepper

4 cups mixed salad greens (such as baby arugula,
     microgreens, or spring mix)

MAKE THE VINAIGRETTE: In a jar with a tight-fitting lid, combine the shallot, vinegar, and olive oil. Shake vigorously until well blended. Season with salt and pepper to taste; refrigerate until needed.

Preheat the oven to 400°F. Sprinkle each beet with a pinch of salt and wrap tightly in a square of aluminum foil. Place the beets on a baking sheet and bake until the centers are tender when pierced with a fork, 45 minutes to 1 hour. Remove from the oven and, when cool enough to handle, peel away the foil. Holding one beet at a time, gently rub off the skin. Cut the peeled beets into ¼-inch dice and set aside at room temperature.

In a stand mixer using the paddle attachment, mix the goat cheese, mascarpone, half of the toasted pine nuts, half of the parsley, one-third of the shallots, and the olive oil. Season with a few pinches of salt and black pepper.

In a small bowl, combine the remaining diced beets, shallots, parsley, and pine nuts with a pinch of salt. Shake the dressing, then toss the beets with 2 tablespoons of the vinaigrette, gradually adding more to taste. In another bowl, dress the salad greens with 1 to 2 tablespoons of the vinaigrette.

TO ASSEMBLE THE SALAD: Place four ring molds, 2¾ inches in diameter and at least 2 inches high, onto four small plates. Divide half of the beet mixture among the rings, packing it lightly in each ring. Divide all the goat cheese mixture among the four rings, packing it lightly and evenly. Top with remaining mixture to fill each mold. Remove the ring mold, top each layered salad with greens, and serve.

Wine pairing Serve this salad with an elegant Chardonnay from Burgundy or a rich Chenin Blanc from Vouvray.

Beet Skewers

MICHAEL ANTHONY

Gramercy Tavern is the essence of colorful New York restaurant life. Owner Danny Meyer, a St. Louis native, was one of the first restaurateurs to carry Bryant Family Vineyard's wines. Chef Michael Anthony plans his daily fare around what's fresh and seasonal. These unusual beet skewers contrast the textures of crispy, crunchy Jerusalem artichokes (also known as sunchokes) with tender, velvety roasted beets, topped with a biting, yet balanced, vinaigrette.

MAKES 18 SKEWERS

BEET SKEWERS

3 medium red beets, roasted

Olive oil

Salt

2 watermelon radishes

10 red radishes

2 sunchokes, peeled

8 sprigs Italian parsley

Extra virgin olive oil to coat,
     plus 1 tablespoon to drizzle

1 tablespoon raspberry vinegar

5 fresh chives, sliced

1 tablespoon *fleur de sel*

BEET VINAIGRETTE

1 tablespoon Montegottero (Sources, see
     page 164) or other raspberry vinegar

1½ teaspoons freshly squeezed lemon juice

1½ teaspoons Pouret (Sources, see page 164)
     or other red wine vinegar

1 cup water

½ cup Terre Bormane (Sources, see page 164)
     or other extra virgin olive oil, plus
     additional as needed

ROAST THE BEETS: Preheat the oven to 400°F. Toss the beets in olive oil (about 2 tablespoons) until generously coated, sprinkle with a pinch of salt, and wrap tightly in a square of aluminum foil. Place the beets on a baking sheet and roast until the centers are tender when pierced with a fork, about 1 hour. Remove from the oven, and when cool enough to handle, peel away the foil. Holding one beet at a time, gently rub off the skin with a paper towel.

MAKE THE VINAIGRETTE: Peel 1 beet and trim the ends. Cut it into chunks and transfer to a blender. Add the raspberry vinegar, lemon juice, red wine vinegar, and water, and purée until smooth. While blending at medium speed, slowly drizzle in the olive oil to form an emulsion. Blend until well combined.

ASSEMBLE THE SKEWERS: Cut the remaining 2 beets crosswise into ¼-inch-thick slices and cut into uniform disks. Set aside.

Thinly slice the watermelon radishes, red radishes, and sunchokes into disks.

Thread the vegetables onto 18 skewers in the following order: beet, parsley leaf, red radish, sunchoke, watermelon radish, beet, red radish, sunchoke, watermelon radish, beet, parsley leaf, red radish. When placing radish slices onto the skewers, fold them in half without breaking them.

Lightly drizzle the skewers with 1 tablespoon olive oil and the raspberry vinegar, and sprinkle with the chives and *fleur de sel.* Pour a small pool of beet vinaigrette on 6 plates, and top with one or more skewers.

Wine pairing What an abundance of flavors and textures! Consider a Chenin Blanc from the Loire Valley, a Kabinett Riesling, or a Gewürztraminer from Alsace. All carry sweet and earthy touches, but can stand up to the varied elements at play.

Belleville White Asparagus and Sunny-Side-Up Duck Eggs

LARRY FORGIONE AND JOSH GALLIANO

Larry Forgione has long been at the forefront of the New American cuisine movement, especially when it comes to championing locally grown food. At his restaurant in downtown St. Louis, An American Place, Larry and *chef de cuisine* Josh Galliano showcase asparagus from Belleville, Illinois, just across the river. Belleville is one of the largest producers of green asparagus and white asparagus in the country. Look for locally grown asparagus at your local farmers' market in the spring. This elegant dish can be served as a first course or a light dinner, or for brunch.

SERVES 4

TEMPURA BATTER

1 cup all-purpose flour

⅓ cup cornstarch

½ cup sparkling water

½ cup beer

BÉARNAISE

¼ cup white wine

¼ cup white wine vinegar

1 sprig tarragon, plus 2 teaspoons
    chopped leaves, for garnish

6 black peppercorns

1 shallot, finely diced

1 cup (2 sticks) unsalted butter

Salt

3 large egg yolks

Ground white pepper

ASPARAGUS VINAIGRETTE

1 tablespoon unsalted butter

1 cup diced shiitake mushroom caps

½ cup diced asparagus (or cut into ½-inch pieces
    if the stalks are thin)

2 tablespoons asparagus vinegar (Sources, see
    page 164) or sherry vinegar

3 tablespoons extra virgin olive oil

Salt and freshly ground black pepper

16 stalks white or green asparagus, peeled

Vegetable oil, for frying

½ cup all-purpose flour, or as needed

½ pound wild asparagus, baby asparagus, or very
    thin asparagus stalks, cut into 3-inch lengths

2 tablespoons olive oil

4 large duck (or chicken) eggs

Sea salt and cracked black pepper

MAKE THE TEMPURA BATTER: Mix the flour and cornstarch together in a mixing bowl. Slowly whisk in the sparkling water and beer until a thin, frothy batter forms. Refrigerate the mixture until ready to use, up to 1 hour.

MAKE THE BÉARNAISE: Combine the white wine, white wine vinegar, tarragon sprig, black peppercorns, and diced shallot in a small saucepan over medium-low heat. Reduce the sauce by half, for about 15 minutes, to a thin syrup-like consistency. Pour though a fine-meshed strainer into a bowl and set aside.

Clarify the butter by slowly melting it in a pot and skimming the foam from the top. Bring a large pot of lightly salted water to a boil, then decrease the heat so the water simmers.

Place the egg yolks and the reduced vinegar syrup in a heatproof mixing bowl large enough to rest on top of the pot with the water. Place the bowl over the simmering water and whisk continuously until the mixture forms stiff ribbons when dropped from a spoon. Remove the bowl from the heat and whisk in the clarified butter. If the mixture feels very stiff, add a few drops of warm water to help loosen the sauce. Season with salt and white pepper to taste, and stir in the chopped tarragon leaves. Set aside and keep warm. Do not discard the pot of simmering water; you can use it to cook the asparagus.

PREPARE THE ASPARAGUS VINAIGRETTE:
Place a small skillet over medium heat and melt
the butter. Add the shiitakes and sauté until
softened and lightly browned. Add the diced
asparagus and sauté until the asparagus just
turns bright green, about 30 seconds more.
Transfer to a small mixing bowl and add the vinegar and olive oil. Season with salt and pepper
to taste, and set aside.

Return the pot of salted water to the heat and
bring to a simmer. Add the asparagus and cook
just until they can be easily pierced with a knife
point, 2 to 3 minutes. Drain, set aside, and
keep warm.

FRY THE ASPARAGUS: Place a small skillet
over medium heat and add 1 inch of vegetable
oil. Remove the tempura batter from the refrigerator. Place the flour in a bowl and dredge the
asparagus in it, then dip in the tempura batter.
Add to the skillet and fry, turning once, until
crispy. Drain on paper towels.

Working quickly, place a sauté pan over medium
heat. Add the olive oil and crack the eggs into
the pan. Allow to sit undisturbed until the egg
whites are cloudy all the way to the yolk.

Place a sunny-side-up egg on each of 4 plates.
Place 4 asparagus stalks on each plate, with the
tips pointing toward the egg, and drizzle the
plate with the vinaigrette. Top the asparagus
with a ribbon of béarnaise, and sprinkle the
egg with sea salt and cracked black pepper.

Wine pairing Asparagus is the perfect
vegetable for an elegant spring brunch. Try a
brut-style California sparkling wine from Napa
or Mendocino to add pizzazz and provide a crisp
balance to the rich béarnaise.

Cheddar Wafers

BARBARA BRYANT

Keep these savory wafers on hand in a tin or in the freezer. You can add another ½ cup of chopped pecans to the dough for an even nuttier flavor.

MAKES ABOUT 12 DOZEN WAFERS

2 cups all-purpose flour

1 teaspoon salt

½ teaspoon cayenne pepper

½ cup (1 stick) unsalted butter,
    at room temperature

2 cups grated sharp or extra-sharp cheddar
    cheese

1 large egg white, beaten with a fork until foamy

1 cup chopped pecans

Wine pairing Pass these delicious wafers around with flutes of dry Champagne or cocktails before dinner.

Using a stand mixer, mix the flour, salt, and cayenne pepper until just combined. Add the butter and cheese and mix well.

Divide the dough into 4 pieces. On a piece of wax paper, roll a piece of dough into a log about 1¼ inches in diameter and 9 inches long. Brush the log with the egg white and roll in the chopped pecans. Repeat with the remaining 3 pieces of dough.

Chill the logs in the refrigerator until firm, about 1 hour.

Preheat the oven to 325°F. Slice each log into ¼-inch-thick pieces, arrange on an ungreased baking sheet, and bake until slightly brown on top, 18 to 20 minutes. Transfer the wafers to wire racks to cool completely. The wafers can be made a day ahead; store in an airtight container, or freeze for up to 1 month.

Blue Cheese Cheesecake

PILAR SANCHEZ

Who says cheesecake should be just for dessert? This rich, savory version can be served with drinks before dinner, a salad for lunch, or as a cheese course at the end of a meal with crisp apple slices.

MAKES ONE 10-INCH CHEESECAKE

(SERVES 12 TO 16 AS AN APPETIZER)

2 cups graham cracker crumbs

½ cup ground toasted walnuts

10 tablespoons (1¼ sticks)
   unsalted butter, melted

2 tablespoons sugar

2 pounds (32 ounces) cream cheese

1½ pounds (24 ounces)
   mascarpone cheese

1 cup sugar

⅔ cup cornstarch

7 large eggs

2 large egg yolks

¾ cup sour cream

⅛ teaspoon vanilla extract

6 ounces (1⅓ cups) crumbled
   Maytag blue cheese

Crostini or toasted baguette slices

Preheat the oven to 300°F. Combine the graham cracker crumbs, walnuts, melted butter, and sugar in a small bowl. Mix thoroughly with a wooden spoon.

Spread and pat down the crust mixture evenly across the bottom of a 10-inch springform pan, going up the sides of the pan no more than 1 inch. Bake for about 6 minutes. Remove from the oven and set aside while you prepare the filling. Decrease the oven temperature to 275°F.

Using a stand mixer, blend the cream cheese, mascarpone, and ½ cup of the sugar together until very smooth. Set aside.

In a small bowl, mix the remaining ½ cup sugar and cornstarch, and add to the cream cheese mixture. With the mixer running, gradually add the eggs, egg yolks, sour cream, vanilla, and blue cheese. Mix until smooth, scraping down the sides of the bowl as necessary. Pour the filling into the prepared crust and bake until set in the center, about 1 hour.

Transfer to a wire rack and allow to cool to room temperature. Refrigerate the cheesecake until chilled, several hours or overnight. Serve cold with crostini.

Wine pairing Pair this with a medium-bodied wine such as a zesty Shiraz from Australia or a fruity Zinfandel. If serving the cheesecake as a cheese course, pair with a late-harvest Riesling or Vidal Blanc from New York or Canada with ripe apricot and honey flavors.

Duck Liver Pâté with Port Aspic

NARSAI DAVID

Luxurious, rich, creamy pâté is always impressive. It's great for the host, too, because it can be made several days in advance. This apple-scented duck liver version is from Narsai David, San Francisco's beloved food and wine guru.

MAKES ABOUT 2 CUPS

DUCK LIVER PÂTÉ

10 tablespoons (1¼ sticks) butter,
    at room temperature

1 small onion, thinly sliced

½ small green apple, peeled and
    thinly sliced

½ pound duck livers

3 tablespoons apple brandy or sherry

2 tablespoons heavy cream

½ teaspoon salt

½ teaspoon freshly squeezed lemon juice

PORT ASPIC

1 teaspoon unflavored powdered gelatin

½ cup port

1 tablespoon sugar

1 tablespoon water

1½ tablespoons red wine vinegar

¼ teaspoon dried tarragon

Baguette slices, for serving

PREPARE THE PÂTÉ: Melt 4 tablespoons of the butter in a large skillet over medium heat. Add the onion and sauté on medium-low heat until soft and brown, about 15 minutes. Add the apple slices and continue to cook until they just start to soften, 3 to 4 minutes. Increase the heat to high and add the duck livers, sautéing until the livers are cooked but still slightly pink in the center. Transfer the mixture to a food processor and set aside.

Add the brandy to the skillet and stir with a wooden spoon, scraping the bottom of the pan. Pour the contents of the pan into the liver mixture and add the cream. Purée the mixture until it is smooth and set it aside to cool to lukewarm.

Put the remaining 6 tablespoons of butter in a mixing bowl and whisk until it is soft. Whisk the liver purée into the butter until fully mixed. Add the salt and lemon juice and blend well. Pack the pâté into a decorative 3-cup terrine or a glass bowl. Set aside to cool.

MAKE THE PORT ASPIC: Sprinkle the gelatin over the port wine in a small bowl, and set aside. Mix the sugar with the water in a small saucepan. Cook over high heat until the sugar melts and turns a medium caramel color; watch carefully, as once the sugar starts to melt it will caramelize very quickly. Remove it immediately from the heat and add the port and gelatin. Return to low heat, add the vinegar and tarragon, and simmer for just 2 minutes. Strain through a fine-meshed sieve and set the aspic aside until it is almost cool.

Pour the aspic over the prepared pâté to make a layer about ⅛ inch thick; if it is too firm to pour, set it in a warm spot or warm briefly in a small pan over very low heat, just enough to thin it. Refrigerate the pâté until the gelatin is firm, at least 1 hour. Serve chilled, with baguette slices.

Wine pairing A rich pâté or foie gras is happily accompanied by an unctuous Sauternes, a Loire Valley Quarts de Chaume, or a Sélection de Grains Nobles Riesling from Alsace.

Mediterranean Tomato-Lemon Tart

DANIEL BOULUD

Daniel Boulud's inspiration to become a chef came from the women in his family—his grandmother and mother—from his native Lyon, France, where the influences of Mediterranean cuisine are strong. I love to serve this tart for lunch, brunch, or a light dinner when summer tomatoes are at their peak with a bowl of seasonal greens seasoned with a lemon and olive oil vinaigrette. Tomatoes, lemons, olives, and garlic are traditional niçoise ingredients.

SERVES 6

TART SHELL

1 cup plus 3 tablespoons all-purpose flour, plus
  additional for dusting

6 tablespoons (¾ stick) cold unsalted butter,
  cut into pieces

Finely grated zest of 1 lemon

⅛ teaspoon salt

1 large egg, lightly beaten

TOMATOES AND LEMON CUSTARD

2 tablespoons extra virgin olive oil

2 cloves garlic, thinly sliced

Leaves from 2 sprigs thyme, chopped

8 plum tomatoes, peeled, halved, and seeded

Salt and freshly ground black pepper

½ cup milk

½ cup heavy cream

2 large eggs

2 large egg yolks

Freshly squeezed juice of 2 lemons

¼ cup pitted niçoise olives

2 tablespoons coarsely chopped basil leaves

MAKE THE TART SHELL: Put the flour, butter, lemon zest, and salt in a food processor and pulse until crumbly. Add the egg and pulse just until moist curds form—don't overprocess. Turn the dough out onto a lightly floured work surface and knead it once or twice so it holds together. Flatten the dough into a disk, wrap in plastic wrap, and refrigerate for at least 1 hour. (Wrapped airtight, the dough can be refrigerated for up to 2 days or frozen for up to 1 month.)

Line a baking sheet with parchment paper. Place an 8-inch tart pan with a removable bottom or a tart ring on the sheet. Lightly dust a work surface and the top of the dough with flour. Using a rolling pin, roll the dough out into a round that is approximately 10 inches in diameter and ⅛ inch thick. As you roll, lift the dough and, if necessary, dust with flour.

Fit the dough into the bottom and against the sides of the pan, taking care not to stretch it. Trim the excess dough even with the pan's rim. If the dough cracks, use lightly moistened scraps to fill the cracks. Refrigerate the dough for at least 30 minutes.

Preheat the oven to 350°F. Top the tart shell with a parchment paper round and fill it with dried beans or rice. Bake for 18 to 20 minutes. Remove the paper and beans, and continue to bake until lightly colored, 3 to 5 minutes more. Transfer to a rack to cool. (The tart shell can be wrapped airtight and kept at room temperature for up to 8 hours.)

COOK THE TOMATOES: Decrease the oven temperature to 300°F. Line a baking sheet with aluminum foil, brush with 1 tablespoon of the oil, and sprinkle with the garlic and thyme. Place the tomato halves, cut side down, on the sheet, sprinkle with the remaining 1 tablespoon oil, and season with salt and pepper to taste. Bake until the tomatoes are tender but still hold their shape, about 1 hour. Set aside.

MAKE THE LEMON CUSTARD: Whisk together the milk, cream, eggs, egg yolks, lemon juice, olives, and basil in a bowl; season with salt and pepper.

Place the tart shell back on the parchment-lined baking sheet, if you have removed it. Arrange the tomatoes, cut side up, in the tart shell and pour the custard mixture over the top. Bake until the custard is set, about 30 minutes. Transfer to a wire rack to cool. To serve, cut the tart into 6 wedges.

Wine pairing A dry rosé from Southern Rhône, such as a chilled Tavel, echoes the fresh and zesty Mediterranean flavors of the tart.

Mushroom Panna Cotta with Wild Mushroom Escabèche

TERRANCE BRENNAN

Terrance Brennan and I met at the Naples Winter Wine Festival. He's a cheery, magnanimous chef who has lots of fun in the kitchen and brings so much creativity to his menus. Escabèche traditionally calls for fish, but this recipe substitutes mushroom-infused panna cotta that is prepared ahead and refrigerated overnight. Once unmolded on serving plates, the chilled custards are surrounded by warm, just-sautéed mushrooms.

SERVES 4

PANNA COTTA

2 tablespoons unsalted butter, plus additional
    for buttering molds

1 shallot, sliced

1 clove garlic, crushed

4 cups chopped mushrooms (such as shiitakes
    and hen-of-the-woods)

3 sprigs thyme

2 tablespoons Madeira

1 cup heavy cream

1 cup milk

2 teaspoons salt

1 tablespoon unflavored powdered gelatin

½ cup cold water

ESCABÈCHE

1 cup extra virgin olive oil

¼ pound assorted mushrooms, thinly sliced

½ cup thinly sliced shallots

1 teaspoon finely chopped garlic

¼ teaspoon ground coriander

½ bay leaf

Finely grated zest of ½ lemon

3 sprigs thyme

¼ cup sherry vinegar

½ teaspoon salt

MAKE THE PANNA COTTA: Butter four 4-ounce (½-cup) ceramic molds or ramekins, and set aside. Melt the 2 tablespoons butter in a saucepan over medium heat. Add the shallot, garlic, mushrooms, and thyme, and sauté until softened, about 5 minutes. Add the Madeira, cream, and milk. Season with salt to taste. Decrease the heat to low and simmer gently for 20 minutes, skimming any foam that rises to the surface. Remove the panna cotta mixture from the heat and set aside.

In a small mixing bowl, dissolve the gelatin in the water. Transfer the panna cotta mixture to a food processor and pulse until blended. Add the gelatin and blend again. Pour the mixture through a fine-meshed strainer into a pitcher or large measuring cup. Divide the mixture among the buttered molds and refrigerate until chilled and firm, at least 4 hours or overnight.

MAKE THE ESCABÈCHE: Heat the olive oil in a medium saucepan. Add the mushrooms, shallots, garlic, coriander, bay leaf, lemon zest, thyme, and vinegar. Sauté until softened, 6 to 8 minutes. Remove the bay leaf and season with the ½ teaspoon salt, or to taste.

Remove the ramekins from the refrigerator and use a butter knife to loosen each panna cotta from its mold. Invert each mold onto the center of a plate. (If the panna cotta doesn't release easily, dip the bottom of the mold into a pan of very hot water for a few seconds.) Divide the escabèche equally around each panna cotta. Serve immediately.

Wine pairing A young, medium-bodied Pinot Noir from Oregon's Willamette Valley or a Village Burgundy are good matches for the woodsy flavors of the wild mushrooms.

Soups and Salads

Calamari and Carrot Salad

MICHAEL ANTHONY

Many Moroccan and Middle Eastern recipes use preserved, or salt-cured, lemons as a condiment. Preserving lemons in salt, lemon juice, and other spices is easy to do, but they must cure for at least 30 days before the lemons are ready to use. Michael Anthony prefers Meyer lemons, but if they are not available, use organic lemons. Preserved lemons are sold in specialty food shops as well.

SERVES 6

PRESERVED MEYER LEMONS

MAKES 10 LEMONS

10 Meyer lemons, well washed

1 tablespoon black peppercorns

1 tablespoon fennel seed

1 tablespoon cumin seed

1 tablespoon coriander seed

1½ cups salt

1 cup sugar

1½ teaspoons hot red pepper flakes

1 star anise

1 cardamom pod

4 cups freshly squeezed lemon juice

LEMON VINAIGRETTE

3 tablespoons Terre Bormane or other
    extra virgin olive oil

1 tablespoon chopped onion

¼ cup freshly squeezed lemon juice

¼ cup lemon-infused olive oil

1½ teaspoons wildflower or other honey

1½ teaspoons white wine vinegar

Salt and freshly ground black pepper

CALAMARI AND CARROT SALAD

2 preserved Meyer lemons, juiced and sliced

½ Meyer lemon rind, sliced

1 head garlic, halved crosswise

1 tablespoon extra virgin olive oil

1 pound calamari, cleaned and bodies cut
    open vertically

Salt and freshly ground black pepper

2 yellow carrots, julienned

2 tablespoons chopped Italian parsley

2 tablespoons toasted pine nuts

Mizuna lettuce or other microgreens,
    for garnish

1½ teaspoons wasabi tobiko

MAKE THE MEYER LEMONS: Cut the lemons lengthwise into quarters, leaving the stem ends intact.

In a small skillet, combine the peppercorns, fennel, cumin, and coriander. Place over high heat, shaking constantly, until toasted and fragrant, about 1 minute. Transfer the spices to a plate and allow to cool.

In a large bowl, mix together the salt, sugar, hot red pepper flakes, star anise, cardamom pod, and toasted spices. Pack the lemons snugly in a large, airtight container, adding the salt mixture along with the lemons so that they are packed tightly in the salt. Cover with lemon juice and secure the lid. Refrigerate for 1 month before using.

MAKE THE LEMON VINAIGRETTE: In a small saucepan, heat 1 tablespoon of the olive oil. Add the onion and sauté until tender but not browned, adding a bit of water if necessary to keep the onion from coloring. Remove from the heat and purée.

In a small bowl, combine the puréed onion, lemon juice, lemon olive oil, honey, and vinegar. Whisk together, slowly drizzling in the remaining 2 tablespoons olive oil to form an emulsion. Season with salt and pepper, and set aside.

MAKE THE CALAMARI: In a large bowl, combine the cured lemons, lemon rind, and garlic. Mix well and set aside. Place a skillet over medium heat and add the olive oil. Season the calamari with salt and pepper, and sauté until just opaque. Remove from the heat and cut the bodies crosswise into julienne. Cut the tentacles into small pieces. Transfer the calamari to the cured lemon mixture and marinate at room temperature for 1 hour.

Add the carrots, parsley, and pine nuts to the calamari. Mix well and mound on a serving platter. Garnish with mizuna lettuce. Stir the wasabi tobiko into the lemon vinaigrette, and drizzle on the plate just before serving.

Wine pairing A young, light white wine such as a Muscadet from the Loire Valley, or a Sauvignon Blanc from northeast Italy, especially Trentino-Alto Adige or Friuli, will bring just the right amount of citrus to match the salad's dressing.

Carrot Soup with Peekytoe Crab Salad and Sweet Pea Crème Fraîche

MATT McGUIRE

Matt McGuire made a name for himself creating cutting edge menus at his St. Louis restaurant, King Louie's. What a great combination of seafood and vegetables he's assembled in this dish. With the mint and honey hints here, follow this first course with the Assyrian Rack of Lamb (page 89). Both dishes are perfect for spring entertaining.

SERVES 4

CARROT SOUP

1 cup (2 sticks) butter

2 medium onions, sliced

3 cloves garlic, chopped

8 large carrots, diced

10 cups carrot juice, or more as needed

1 jalapeño pepper, halved and seeded

Salt and freshly ground black pepper

SWEET PEA CRÈME FRAÎCHE

1 cup blanched fresh peas

1 cup crème fraîche

1 tablespoon honey

Juice of ½ orange

Salt and freshly ground black pepper

PEEKYTOE CRAB SALAD

½ pound peekytoe or other crabmeat

¼ cup minced red onion

1 tablespoon chopped fresh mint leaves

½ jalapeño pepper, seeded and minced

2 tablespoons chopped Italian parsley

3 tablespoons mascarpone cheese

Salt and freshly ground black pepper

MAKE THE CARROT SOUP: Melt the butter in a large wide pot over medium-low heat, and add the onions and garlic. Cover and cook, stirring occasionally, until the onions are soft and translucent.

Add the diced carrots. Cover and cook until the carrots are partially tender. Add the carrot juice and the jalapeño, and simmer until soft. Using a blender, purée until very smooth. Strain through a chinois or fine-meshed strainer. Season with salt and pepper. If the soup is too thick, thin it with additional carrot juice as needed.

ASSEMBLE THE CRAB SALAD: In a medium bowl, combine the crabmeat, red onion, mint, jalapeño, parsley, and mascarpone. Toss well to mix, and season with salt and pepper to taste. Cover and refrigerate until serving.

MAKE THE SWEET PEA CRÈME FRAÎCHE: Bring a small pan of water to a boil. Add the peas and simmer until they are bright green and tender. Drain well and rinse under cold water to cool. Transfer the peas to a blender and add the crème fraîche, honey, and orange juice. Purée until smooth. Press the peas through a chinois or fine-meshed strainer, and season with salt and pepper.

Place an equal portion of crab salad in the center of 4 large soup plates. Pour the soup around the salad, and garnish with the sweet pea crème fraîche.

Wine pairing The shellfish and tender, sweet vegetables make white Châteauneuf-du-Pape or a Viognier a good choice for this dish.

Chilled Pea Soup

BILL CARDWELL

Fresh thyme and dill make this chilled pea soup particularly refreshing. I suggest serving this with homemade toast points made from brioche or challah.

SERVES 4

2 teaspoons olive oil

1 cup sliced shallots

2 pounds fresh or frozen green peas

4 cups vegetable stock

1 sprig thyme

¼ cup sour cream

1 teaspoon fresh dill

2 teaspoons cider vinegar

Salt and freshly ground white pepper

1 tablespoon finely diced carrot

9 snow peas, julienned

1 tablespoon truffle oil

Place the olive oil in a heavy pot over medium heat. Add the shallots and cook until soft and translucent.

Add the peas, vegetable stock, and thyme. If using fresh peas, bring the stock to a boil and simmer for a minute or two to remove the raw flavor, then let cool. If using frozen peas, bring to a boil, remove immediately from the heat, and let cool.

Remove and discard the thyme. Place the peas and stock in a blender. Add the sour cream, dill, and vinegar and purée until very smooth. Pass the mixture though a fine-meshed strainer to remove the pea shells. Season with salt and white pepper to taste. Cover and refrigerate until well chilled.

To serve, toss the carrots and snow peas with the truffle oil in a large bowl. Ladle the soup into bowls or soup plates, and garnish with the carrots and snow peas.

Wine pairing With this chilled soup, enjoy a Graves-style Sauvignon/Sémillon blend, a Rueda from Spain, or a Verdicchio from Italy.

Wild Mushroom Soup

BERNARD DERVIEUX

A meal unto itself, this fragrant soup can be prepared a day or two in advance. For a lower-calorie version, use low-fat milk instead of cream. Fill a basket with plenty of rustic artisanal bread for mopping up every bit of the soup.

SERVES 4

3 tablespoons butter

2 shallots, finely chopped

2 cups fresh shiitake, chanterelle, or other wild
mushrooms, coarsely chopped

4 cups chicken stock

2 tablespoons heavy cream

Salt and freshly ground black pepper

Place a large deep skillet or saucepan over medium-low heat. Melt 1 tablespoon of the butter, add the shallots, and sauté until translucent. Stir in the mushrooms and sauté until just wilted, 2 to 3 minutes.

Add the chicken stock and simmer until the mushrooms are tender, 7 to 10 minutes. Remove from the heat and allow the soup to cool until no longer steaming.

Using a blender or food processor, blend until smooth but not completely puréed. Specks of mushrooms should still be visible.

Return the soup to the saucepan. Bring to a simmer over medium-low heat, add the cream, and bring back to a simmer. Turn off the heat, and stir in the remaining 2 tablespoons butter until it is melted. Season with salt and pepper to taste. Serve hot.

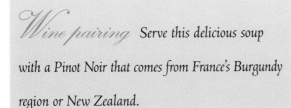 *Wine pairing* *Serve this delicious soup with a Pinot Noir that comes from France's Burgundy region or New Zealand.*

Feta-Orzo Salad

TERRANCE BRENNAN

Terrance serves this salad with the simple grilled chicken on page 97. It's a perfect picnic salad as well.

SERVES 4

6 ripe plum tomatoes

¾ cup plus 1 tablespoon extra virgin olive oil

1 tablespoon finely chopped garlic

½ teaspoon fresh thyme leaves

½ teaspoon kosher salt

½ cup peeled and diced eggplant

½ cup diced fennel

½ cup diced zucchini

Salt

1½ cups orzo

1 cup niçoise olives, pitted

2 cups packed arugula

1 cup (about 6 ounces) crumbled feta cheese

2 tablespoons red wine vinegar

Crushed black peppercorns

Preheat the oven to 200°F. Cut the tomatoes in half lengthwise, squeeze out the seeds, and cut in half again lengthwise. Transfer to a bowl and toss with 2 tablespoons of the olive oil, the garlic, thyme, and ½ teaspoon kosher salt.

Line a baking sheet with aluminum foil, set a wire cooling rack on top of it, and place the tomatoes on the rack. Roast the tomatoes until dry but still a bit supple, about 2½ hours. The tomatoes at the outer edges of the rack might cook more quickly, so use tongs to move them as necessary to ensure they cook evenly. When the tomatoes are cool enough to handle, remove the skins with a paring knife and discard. (The tomatoes can be refrigerated in an airtight container for up to 3 days.)

Place a medium sauté pan over medium heat and allow to heat for 1 minute. Add 2 tablespoons of the olive oil, the eggplant, fennel, zucchini, and salt to taste. Sauté until tender but not browned, about 8 minutes. Remove the pan from the heat and allow to cool.

Fill a large bowl halfway with ice water. Fill a medium saucepan with water and add 1 tablespoon salt. Place over medium-high heat and bring to a boil. Add the orzo, stir, and cook until tender, approximately 4 minutes. Drain well, then place in the ice water. Drain again and toss with 1 tablespoon of the olive oil. Transfer the orzo to a baking sheet and spread it out so that it cools as quickly as possible. (Once cooled, the orzo can be refrigerated in an airtight container for up to 24 hours.)

To assemble the salad, place the orzo in a large bowl. Add the sautéed vegetables, roasted tomatoes, olives, arugula, and feta. In a separate bowl, make a vinaigrette by whisking together the remaining ½ cup olive oil, red wine vinegar, ½ teaspoon salt, and a pinch of crushed black pepper. Pour ¾ of the vinaigrette into the bowl with the orzo salad, and toss gently to mix.

To serve, place equal amounts of arugula in the center of each plate. Spoon a quarter of the orzo salad in the center of the arugula, taking care to include a few tomato quarters on each plate. Drizzle the plates with the remaining vinaigrette, and serve.

Wine pairing A new level of quality wines has started to emerge from Greece, and if you can find them locally, try a Moschofilero or Assyrtiko. Both are dry, crisp white grapes that will pair with the feta. If unavailable, serve a zesty Sancerre.

Lobster Salad with Haricots Verts

BERNARD DERVIEUX

A special occasion—birthday or anniversary—calls for this elegant lobster salad. The lobsters and beans can be prepared ahead, and everything can be assembled at the last moment.

SERVES 4

12 cups water

1 stalk celery, cut into large pieces

1 carrot, cut into large pieces

½ onion

2 cups dry white wine

½ cup white vinegar

1 sprig thyme

1 bay leaf

1 teaspoon salt

1 teaspoon black peppercorns

2 (1½- to 2-pound) live lobsters

1 pound haricots verts
   (small French green beans), trimmed

1 shallot, diced

2 tablespoons heavy cream

1 tablespoon freshly squeezed lemon juice

1 tablespoon chopped fresh tarragon

2 tablespoons unsalted butter

Ground white pepper

In a large stockpot, combine 3 quarts water, the celery, carrot, onion, 1 cup of the wine, vinegar, thyme, bay leaf, salt, and peppercorns. Boil, uncovered, for 15 minutes. Add the lobsters to the pot, return to a boil, and cook for 12 minutes. Reserve 1 cup of the cooking liquid, then drain the lobsters and allow them to cool. When the lobsters are cool enough to handle, remove their meat. Cut the lobster meat into large pieces, cover, and refrigerate until needed.

Fill a 4-quart saucepan with lightly salted water, place over high heat, and bring to a boil. Meanwhile, fill a large bowl with ice water and set aside. Add the haricots verts to the boiling water, and cook until bright green and tender, 2 to 3 minutes, tasting one to ensure its tenderness. Drain and immediately plunge the beans into the ice water. Drain again and set aside.

In a large saucepan, combine the shallot, the reserved 1 cup lobster stock, and the remaining 1 cup wine. Place over high heat and reduce to ½ cup. Add the cream and return to a simmer. Add the lemon juice, tarragon, and butter. Season with salt and white pepper to taste. Add the lobster meat and allow it to warm in the sauce for 1 minute.

To serve, mound equal portions of lobster in the center of 4 serving plates, and surround with the haricots verts. Ladle the warm sauce over the lobster and beans, and serve immediately.

Wine pairing *Sommeliers often talk about the "flavor profile" of a recipe. Using the profile, they suggest wines that counterpoint or complement flavors. For this salad, an elegant Chardonnay from the Los Carneros region of southern Sonoma and Napa has just the right profile—elegant ripe fruit of apples with hints of vanilla and spice backed up with enough acid to help carry the rich, sweet lobster.*

Minestrone di Branzino

LIDIA BASTIANICH

Lidia is the personification of food, family, and friends sharing and enjoying life together. Eating at her restaurant in New York is always a pleasure. This sea bass and couscous soup captures the light, fresh flavors so characteristic of her native Italy.

SERVES 8

1 (2-pound) branzino (sea bass), filleted and
  skinned, head and bones reserved for stock

12 cups water

2 stalks celery, cut into 1-inch pieces

1 carrot, sliced

4 cloves garlic, crushed

2 bay leaves

10 black peppercorns

1 cup shredded carrots

¼ cup extra virgin olive oil, plus more for
  drizzling

2 cups (6 to 8) shredded baby zucchini

3 cups fresh or canned whole, peeled plum
  tomatoes

1 teaspoon hot red pepper flakes

Coarse sea salt

½ cup fine-grain couscous

Place the fish head and bones in a large, wide saucepan, and add the water. Add the celery, sliced carrot, garlic, bay leaves, and peppercorns. Bring to a simmer over medium-low heat and cook gently for 30 minutes. Strain and reserve the broth, and reserve any good pieces of fish from the head for garnishing.

While the fish broth is simmering, sauté the shredded carrots in the olive oil until wilted, approximately 5 minutes. Add the zucchini and continue cooking for 2 minutes. Crush the tomatoes coarsely with your hands and stir into the zucchini-carrot mixture. Add the red pepper flakes and salt to taste; bring to a boil, then add the fish broth. Cook for 20 minutes at a gentle, rolling boil.

Cut the fish into 1- by ½-inch pieces and add to the soup. Continue to cook for 7 minutes, until the fish is opaque. Add the couscous and cook for another 2 minutes. Taste and adjust the seasoning as necessary. Serve in bowls with an additional drizzle of extra virgin olive oil.

Wine pairing A dry rosé or rosato provides a great counterpoint to the tomatoes yet sustains enough body to hold its own with the couscous and vegetables. Lidia, by the way, makes a wonderful rosato from Refosco grapes.

Summer Salad

DAN BARBER

The fresh-from-the-farm philosophy (whether the food is from its own farm or from other local sources) makes Blue Hill at Stone Barns a one-of-a-kind restaurant in New York State's Hudson Valley. While Chef Dan Barber heads up the restaurant, there is also an education center devoted to promoting a deeper connection between the land, the farmer, and the diner. Blue Hill at Stone Barns makes this salad with eggs, greens, and herbs raised outside the kitchen door.

SERVES 6

LEMON OIL

4 cups canola oil

Zest of ½ lemon, removed in strips

¼ cup packed fresh lemon thyme

¼ stalk lemongrass

LEMON VINAIGRETTE

½ teaspoon Dijon mustard

¼ cup freshly squeezed lemon juice

½ cup olive oil

Salt and freshly ground black pepper

SALAD

3 cups mixed micro- or baby greens (such as arugula, beet greens, baby kale, and mesclun)

1 cup mixed fresh herbs (such as Italian parsley, tarragon, chervil, thyme, mint, cilantro, and chives)

½ cup shelled roasted pistachios

⅓ cup dried apricots, diced

ALMOND SOFT-FRIED EGGS

6 large eggs

¼ cup all-purpose flour

1 teaspoon kosher salt

½ teaspoon freshly ground black pepper

2 large eggs, lightly beaten

¾ cup panko (Japanese bread crumbs)

½ cup finely ground almonds

½ cup freshly grated Parmigiano-Reggiano cheese

Peanut or vegetable oil, for frying

MAKE THE LEMON OIL: In a medium saucepan, combine the canola oil, lemon zest, lemon thyme, and lemongrass. Place over very low heat for 1 hour; do not let the oil simmer. Remove from the heat, let cool, and strain. Refrigerate until needed. Use remaining oil as a base for salad dressings or marinades.

PREPARE THE LEMON VINAIGRETTE:

Whisk the mustard and lemon juice together in a bowl. Whisk in ¼ cup of the lemon oil, reserving the remainder for another use. Whisk in the olive oil, and season with salt and pepper to taste.

In a large bowl, toss together the greens, herbs, pistachios, and apricots. Refrigerate until needed.

MAKE THE ALMOND SOFT-FRIED EGGS:

Bring a medium pot of water to a boil, gently add the whole eggs, and cook for 6 minutes. Immediately remove the eggs and immerse in a bowl of ice water until cold. Carefully peel the eggs and set aside.

In the first of 3 medium bowls, combine the flour, ½ teaspoon of the salt, and ¼ teaspoon of the pepper. In the second bowl, whisk the beaten eggs until smooth. In the third bowl, combine the panko, ground almonds, Parmesan, the remaining ½ teaspoon salt, and the remaining ¼ teaspoon pepper.

To coat the eggs, first roll the cold, soft-cooked eggs in the flour, shaking to remove any excess. Dip the eggs into the beaten egg mixture, then in the panko mixture, rolling until completely coated. Repeat with a second coating of beaten egg and crumb mixture, pressing the crumb mixture around the eggs to secure the coating. (If desired, the coated eggs may be covered and refrigerated for up to 4 hours.)

To cook the coated eggs, clip a deep-fry thermometer to the side of a medium saucepan. Fill the pot with about 3 inches of oil and heat to 350°F. Add the eggs and cook, turning, until golden brown and heated through, about 2 minutes. Remove from the oil and drain on paper towels.

To serve, dress the salad with the lemon vinaigrette. Divide equal portions of the salad among 6 bowls and top each serving with an almond-fried egg.

Wine pairing With the lemon vinaigrette, you'll want a light, citrusy wine. A white Bordeaux from France or a Verdelho from Spain will round out all the flavors.

Fish and Shellfish

Grilled Halibut with Spinach and Caper-Lemon Sauce

VINCE P. BOMMARITO

Tony's, a beloved landmark in St. Louis, has repeatedly won a coveted Mobil four-star rating. Vince, the founder, and his son Vince are masterful chefs, especially when preparing fish and shellfish. Mild-flavored halibut is first marinated in olive oil, garlic, and basil and then coated in bread crumbs before grilling. The fish is served on a bed of spinach with a touch of hot red pepper flakes and caper-lemon sauce.

SERVES 4

2 tablespoons extra virgin olive oil

2 large cloves garlic, finely chopped

1 tablespoon chopped fresh basil

1 teaspoon salt

½ teaspoon freshly ground black pepper

4 (7-ounce) halibut fillets, skinned

1 cup fresh white bread crumbs

CAPER-LEMON SAUCE

¼ cup extra virgin olive oil

¼ cup freshly squeezed lemon juice

1½ tablespoons capers, lightly crushed

1 small clove garlic, finely chopped

1½ teaspoons chopped fresh basil

Salt and freshly ground black pepper

SPINACH

4 tablespoons (½ stick) unsalted butter

½ teaspoon hot red pepper flakes

2 pounds spinach, stemmed

Salt

Mix together the olive oil, garlic, basil, salt, and pepper in a shallow pan large enough to hold the fish in one layer. Add the halibut fillets, turning to coat well. Cover and refrigerate for 1 hour.

Whisk together the olive oil, lemon juice, capers, garlic, and basil in a small bowl. Season with salt and pepper to taste. Set aside.

Melt the butter in a large, deep pot over medium-low heat. Stir in the pepper flakes. Add the spinach. Cook, stirring frequently, until the spinach is wilted, about 5 minutes. Season with salt to taste. Set aside, keeping warm.

Preheat a grill. Remove the fish from the refrigerator and dredge both sides in the bread crumbs. Decrease the heat to medium and cook the fish until it is lightly browned on the outside and opaque and flaky in the center, about 3 minutes per side.

Divide the spinach among 4 large plates, and arrange the halibut on top of the spinach. Stir the sauce well, spoon over the halibut, and serve.

Wine pairing A crisp, white Sauvignon Blanc from Pouilly-Fumé or a Vernaccia di San Gimignano will respond nicely to the bold green flavors of the spinach and the capers.

Grilled Salmon with Cabernet-Coriander Onions and Potato-Watercress Salad

BRYAN CARR

When I asked Bryan Carr for a recipe that would go well with Cabernet Sauvignon, he took my request seriously! This salmon dish, accented with wine-infused onions, pungent coriander, and savory watercress, provides a great combination of flavors, colors, and textures. Bryan's presence is a great addition to the St. Louis restaurant scene. His two restaurants are located between my home and my office, making it convenient to stop by for breakfast, lunch, or dinner, which I often do.

SERVES 6

CABERNET-CORIANDER ONIONS

1 tablespoon freshly ground coriander seeds

2 tablespoons unsalted butter

3 large yellow onions, thinly sliced

1 bay leaf

Freshly ground black pepper

2 cups Cabernet Sauvignon or other
    dry red wine

POTATO-WATERCRESS SALAD

1½ pounds Yukon gold potatoes

¼ cup red wine vinegar

¼ cup whole-grain mustard

1 medium shallot, thinly sliced

1 cup hazelnut, peanut, or olive oil

Salt and freshly ground black pepper

2 bunches (about 4 cups) watercress

½ cup sliced fresh chives

SALMON

Extra virgin olive oil

6 (6-ounce) salmon fillets

Salt and freshly ground black pepper

Lemon wedges, for garnish

PREPARE THE ONIONS: Place the coriander seeds in a small, dry skillet over high heat, shaking the pan often until the seeds are fragrant, 1 to 2 minutes. Using a spice grinder or mortar and pestle, grind to a fine powder.

Melt the butter in a large heavy saucepan over medium heat. Add the onions, coriander, bay leaf, and a few grindings of black pepper. Sauté until the onions soften. Add the wine, raise the heat to high, and bring the wine to a boil, stirring occasionally, until the wine evaporates and the onions are a deep red wine color. Set the onions aside at room temperature, or cover tightly and refrigerate for up to 24 hours.

MAKE THE POTATO SALAD: Peel the potatoes, place in a large pot, and cover with cold water. Bring to a boil and cook until the potatoes are just tender. Drain and plunge into cold water. As soon as the potatoes are cool enough to handle, drain again and reserve.

Make the salad dressing by whisking together the vinegar, mustard, and shallot in a bowl. Add the oil in a slow stream, whisking it in as you go. Season with salt and pepper to taste.

Remove the leaves from one bunch of watercress. Thinly slice the potatoes, about ⅓ inch thick. Mix together the potatoes, watercress, chives, and dressing in a large

serving bowl. You may have more dressing than you need; if so, reserve for another use. Cover and refrigerate until serving; the salad is best prepared 2 to 4 hours in advance.

GRILL THE SALMON: Wipe the grill grate with olive oil. Preheat the grill to high. Meanwhile, reheat the onions and bring the potato salad to room temperature. Rub each of the salmon fillets lightly with olive oil and a sprinkling of salt and pepper. Grill the salmon for about 3 minutes on each side.

To serve, divide the remaining 1 bunch of watercress among 6 plates. On one side of the watercress place a small mound of potato salad. On the other side, place the onions on top of the watercress. Finally, top each mound of onions with a salmon fillet. Garnish with lemon wedges.

Wine pairing While Pinot Noirs have become the classic pairing for grilled salmon, a rich but crisp Pinot Gris from Oregon can complement the salmon and counter the peppery watercress. A Grenache-based dry rosé can also be an interesting alternative.

Oyster Poor Boys

KEVIN NASHAN

Kevin Nashan brings the flavors of New Orleans up the Mississippi to his St. Louis restaurant, the Sydney Street Cafe. The crunchiness of the fried oysters and the truffle aioli elevate this New Orleans classic to a new level of sophistication.

SERVES 6

AS AN APPETIZER OR FIRST COURSE

TRUFFLE AIOLI

1 large egg

3 large egg yolks

2 tablespoons white wine vinegar

2 teaspoons dry mustard

2 ¼ cups vegetable oil

⅓ cup truffle oil (optional)

2 tablespoons freshly squeezed lemon juice

Salt and freshly ground black pepper

12 dry-packed sun-dried tomatoes

1 cup packed Italian parsley leaves

⅓ cup vegetable oil

2 tablespoons truffle oil (optional)

Salt

4 cups vegetable oil, or as needed,
for deep frying

⅓ cup all-purpose flour

2 to 3 teaspoons cayenne pepper

12 large oysters, such as Blue Point, shucked

Salt and freshly ground black pepper

12 (2-inch-square) pieces white bread, toasted

12 small arugula leaves

MAKE THE TRUFFLE AIOLI: In the bowl of a food processor, combine the egg, egg yolks, vinegar, and dry mustard and pulse to blend. With the motor running, very slowly drizzle in the vegetable oil until it is fully incorporated and the mixture is thick. Drizzle in the truffle oil and lemon juice and season with salt and pepper to taste. Remove to a bowl, cover, and refrigerate until needed.

Cover the sun-dried tomatoes with boiling water and allow to sit for 20 minutes. Meanwhile, to make the parsley *jus,* fill a large bowl with ice water and set aside. Bring a medium saucepan of water to a boil and add the parsley leaves. Blanch for 15 seconds, then drain quickly and with a skimmer transfer the parsley to the ice water.

As soon as the parsley is chilled, drain it well and transfer to a blender or food processor. Pulse until chopped. With the motor running, slowly drizzle in the vegetable oil until the mixture is smooth. Add the truffle oil, and season with a pinch of salt. Transfer to a bowl and set aside.

FRY THE OYSTERS: Using a deep fryer with a candy or deep-fry thermometer clipped to the side, heat the vegetable oil to 325°F. Combine the flour and cayenne in a bowl. Just before frying, dredge the oysters in the flour-cayenne mixture and shake off any excess. Deep-fry the oysters until the exteriors are brown and crunchy, 45 to 60 seconds. Do not crowd the pan, or the oil temperature will decrease, causing the oysters to become soggy rather than crisp. Remove the oysters with a wire strainer and drain on paper towels. Season with salt and black pepper to taste.

To serve, spread each square of toasted bread with truffle aioli. Top with a sun-dried tomato half and an arugula leaf. Place a fried oyster on top, then a small dollop more of aioli. Garnish with 1 teaspoon of parsley *jus,* and serve immediately.

Wine pairing A citrusy Sauvignon Blanc from the Spanish grape Verdejo, which is often blended with Sauvignon Blanc, is an excellent counterpoint to the battered oyster. An Italian Cortese di Gavi (from the home of truffles) also offers the fresh, light fruits of lemon-lime.

Marinated Yellowfin Tuna with Roasted Beets, Radish, and Lemon Oil

RICK REDDINGTON

Rick Reddington is a master at preparing seafood and loves to include baby vegetables in his recipes. They're bound to be the freshest, and they have more delicate flavors than mature varieties. Everything in this dish can be prepared ahead and then assembled at the last minute. Make sure to purchase sushi-grade tuna.

SERVES 4 TO 6

1 bunch baby gold beets

1 bunch baby red beets

1 bunch baby Chioggia beets (if not available, substitute baby red beets)

Salt and freshly ground black pepper

Extra virgin olive oil

½ pound sushi-grade tuna loin, cut into 2-inch pieces

LEMON VINAIGRETTE

¼ cup freshly squeezed lemon juice (1 to 2 large lemons)

¼ to ½ cup extra virgin olive oil

Salt and freshly ground black pepper

Fleur de sel

½ cup Agrumato or other lemon-infused extra virgin olive oil (Sources, see page 164)

1 small shallot, peeled and finely diced

1 bunch chives, finely sliced

5 French breakfast radishes, trimmed

1 bunch cilantro, stems discarded and leaves cut into chiffonade

ROAST THE BEETS: Preheat the oven to 325°F. Trim the tops of the gold beets, red beets, and Chioggia beets, leaving about ¼ inch of the stems attached. Toss with salt, pepper, and olive oil, and place in a shallow roasting pan. Cover tightly with aluminum foil and roast until knife-tender, 35 to 40 minutes. Let cool slightly. Peel while still warm by holding the beets in a paper towel and gently pinching the skins; they should easily slip off. Remove the stems, cut into quarters, and reserve.

PREPARE THE TUNA: Place the tuna on a sheet of plastic wrap. Moisten with olive oil. Place another sheet of plastic wrap on top of the tuna. Gently pound with a kitchen mallet or the bottom of a cast-iron skillet until evenly flattened. Repeat with each piece of tuna. Chill until ready to assemble.

MAKE THE LEMON VINAIGRETTE: In a small bowl, combine the lemon juice and olive oil, and whisk until blended. Season with salt and pepper to taste. Reserve.

Remove the top layer of plastic wrap from the tuna and invert onto a chilled 12-inch plate. Season the tuna with *fleur de sel* and freshly ground pepper. Drizzle lightly with lemon oil (1 to 2 tablespoons per piece). Dress the beets with diced shallots, half of the chives, salt, pepper, and about ½ cup of the lemon vinaigrette. Spoon onto the tuna in little mounds.

Slice the radishes thinly (they should be almost translucent) on a mandoline or with a sharp knife. Drop onto the beets. Drizzle a little lemon vinaigrette (about ¾ teaspoon) over each piece of tuna and garnish with the remaining chives and the cilantro chiffonade.

Wine pairing A citrusy New Zealand Sauvignon Blanc is a racy match for the tart lemon vinaigrette. For a little less intensity, try a white Graves from Bordeaux.

Sautéed Diver Scallops with Cauliflower, Capers, and Almonds

RICK REDDINGTON

Rick Reddington calls for a special kind of scallop for this recipe: divers plunge into the cold Atlantic waters and hand-pluck these large scallops from the rocks, leaving the small ones behind to continue growing. Chefs prefer diver scallops because of their freshness, natural plumpness, and eco-friendly harvesting. They can be hard to find, but any large sea scallops, not the smaller bay scallops, can be substituted.

**SERVES 4 AS A FIRST COURSE,
OR 2 AS A MAIN COURSE**

½ cup balsamic vinegar

Salt

2 cups 1½-inch cauliflower florets

¼ cup heavy cream

1 tablespoon extra virgin olive oil

8 diver scallops, or large sea scallops

Freshly ground black pepper

1½ tablespoons unsalted butter

2 tablespoons capers

2 tablespoons slivered almonds

2 tablespoons golden raisins

1 tablespoon chopped Italian parsley

Bring the balsamic vinegar to a boil in a small saucepan and reduce by about half; it should be thick but still pourable. Set aside.

In a large pot, bring 2 quarts of lightly salted water to a boil. Set aside a large bowl of ice water. Add 1 cup of the cauliflower to the boiling water and blanch until tender, about 1 minute. Drain, plunge the florets into the ice water until chilled, and then drain again.

Combine the uncooked cauliflower and cream in a medium saucepan over medium-low heat and simmer until very soft, about 8 minutes. Purée in a food processor or blender, and press through a fine-meshed sieve into a warm bowl. Cover and keep warm.

Warm 2 small (about 7-inch) sauté pans. Add the olive oil to one pan. Season the scallops with salt and pepper. When the oil just starts to smoke, add the scallops. Cook, turning once, until the scallops are lightly colored (medium-rare) on both sides, about 1 minute per side, depending on the thickness of the scallops. In the other pan, melt the butter and allow it to begin to brown. Add the blanched florets and sauté for 1 minute. Add the capers, almonds, raisins, and parsley and mix well. Season with salt and pepper to taste.

To serve, pour a small circle of the cauliflower puree in the middle of each warmed plate. Add a portion of the caper mixture in the center, and top with 2 scallops. Drizzle the balsamic vinegar reduction around the plate and garnish with a drizzle of extra virgin olive oil. Serve immediately.

Wine pairing A light, slightly chilled Beaujolais will help bridge the earthy-salty flavors of the cauliflower and capers, and will call attention to the tender sweetness of the scallops.

Slow-Baked Wild Salmon with Chanterelle Vinaigrette

TERRANCE BRENNAN

To appreciate Terrance's recipe to the fullest, he recommends the best-quality wild salmon you can find. Yes, wild salmon is more expensive than farm raised, but the taste is worth it.

SERVES 4

CHANTERELLE VINAIGRETTE

4 cups chicken stock

2 tablespoons white wine vinegar

1½ teaspoons salt

1 cup extra virgin olive oil

2 medium shallots, finely diced

1 teaspoon chopped garlic

½ pound chanterelle mushrooms, quartered

3 sprigs thyme

4 (5- to 6-ounce) wild salmon fillets

2 tablespoons extra virgin olive oil

1 sprig thyme

1 clove garlic, thinly sliced

MAKE THE CHANTERELLE VINAIGRETTE:
Place the chicken stock in a saucepan over medium-high heat and boil until reduced to ½ cup, approximately 30 minutes. Let cool. Add the vinegar and salt. Using an immersion blender, or by hand with a whisk, add in ¾ cup of the oil until well blended.

Heat the remaining ¼ cup olive oil in a sauté pan over medium heat. Add the shallots and sauté until translucent. Add the garlic, chanterelles, and thyme and sauté until tender, 5 to 6 minutes. Remove the pan from the heat and allow to cool until the mushrooms are just warm. Add the mixture to the vinaigrette, and set aside.

Preheat the oven to 250°F. Arrange the salmon in a baking dish large enough to hold the fillets in a single layer. In a small bowl, combine the olive oil, thyme, and garlic. Pour over the salmon. Bake the salmon until cooked to taste, 25 to 35 minutes for medium-rare.

To serve, place a salmon fillet in the center of each of 4 plates. Whisk the vinaigrette until well blended and pour over the fillets. Serve immediately.

Wine pairing Wild salmon is naturally rich; chanterelles are naturally earthy. Both flavors will be enhanced by a Pinot Noir from the Northwest. For a lighter touch, serve a Pinot Noir rosé or a Blanc de Noir.

Smoked Salmon Croque Monsieur

ERIC RIPERT

Eric Ripert's innovative riff on the classic croque monsieur is perfect for lunch or a light meal. For a bit of luxury, spread caviar on top of the Gruyère before grilling. Eric's lemon confit is simple to make, but allow at least a month for curing. Once you have it in your pantry, you will find it's as versatile as vinegar, salt, or a spice.

SERVES 6

LEMON CONFIT

6 lemons

3 cups kosher salt

12 (½-inch-thick) slices Pullman bread or
    other good-quality white bread

¾ pound thinly sliced smoked salmon

1 tablespoon Lemon Confit, cut into tiny dice

1 tablespoon sliced fresh chives

6 ounces Gruyère cheese, sliced as thinly
    as possible on a mandoline or with a
    vegetable peeler

4 tablespoons (½ stick) unsalted butter,
    at room temperature

MAKE THE CONFIT: Sterilize a one-quart jar in boiling water, and then dry upside down on a rack. Pour a layer of salt in the bottom of the jar once it has dried.

Cut 1 inch off the end of each lemon. Quarter each lemon starting at the cut side, but leaving the uncut side intact. Over a bowl, open a lemon and pour salt inside. Place the lemon in the bottom of the jar. Continue with the remaining lemons, using the salt that falls into the bowl. Pack the lemons in the jar, covering each layer with salt. Seal the jar with a tight-fitting lid and refrigerate. (The lemons are ready after 1 month. They are best after 3 months and will keep for a year or more in a dark cupboard.)

To use, wash the salt from the lemons and slice to desired thickness. If the lemons are not going to be cooked with the dish they are seasoning— for example, sprinkled on a salad or on smoked salmon—then they should be blanched in water to remove the salt.

Place 6 of the bread slices on a work surface. Top each slice with an equal portion of the smoked salmon. Sprinkle the salmon with the lemon confit and chives. Top with the Gruyère and the remaining 6 slices of bread. Using a serrated knife, cut off the crusts. The croque monsieur can be covered with plastic wrap and refrigerated for up to 2 hours.

Before serving, spread the outsides of the sandwiches with the softened butter. Preheat a large nonstick frying pan over medium-high heat. Add the sandwiches to the pan with the Gruyère sides closest to the heat and sauté until golden brown, about 2 minutes. Turn them over and brown on the other side, about 1 minute.

To serve, quarter each croque monsieur diagonally to make 4 triangles. Arrange on 4 serving plates, and serve immediately.

Wine pairing Pinot Gris from Alsace has lemon-lime and nutty flavors and just the right acidity to cut through the rich Gruyère and smoked salmon.

Tilapia with Beurre Blanc aux Champignons

JAMES FIALA

Although Jimmy prepares many outstanding dishes, I find myself ordering this one time after time. The spinach and mushrooms create a perfect bed for this mild white fish. Jimmy adds: "Sounds fancy, but we maintain our theory that simple is better with this flavorful Crossing favorite. The dish revolves around the velvety rich mushroom sauce. Any white-flesh fish, such as sole or flounder, cooked in any fashion, can be substituted for tilapia."

SERVES 6

5 tablespoons extra virgin olive oil

1 large shallot, sliced

10 white mushrooms, sliced

2 large portobello mushrooms, sliced

10 shiitake mushrooms, sliced

Salt and freshly ground black pepper

⅔ cup dry vermouth

1 (750-milliliter) bottle Chablis or other dry
    white wine

1 teaspoon cornstarch (optional)

1½ cups (3 sticks) unsalted butter, cut into
    small cubes

6 tilapia fillets

In a large saucepan over low heat, combine 3 tablespoons of the olive oil and the shallot. Cover and cook until the shallot is soft but not browned, about 3 minutes. Increase the heat to high, and add the white, portobello, and shiitake mushrooms. Cover and cook, stirring about once a minute, until the volume of mushrooms reduces by half, about 5 minutes; be very careful not to burn the bottom of the pot. Season with a couple of pinches of salt and pepper.

Add the vermouth and the wine to the mushrooms and boil, uncovered, until reduced to about ¾ cup, then decrease the heat to medium-low. For a creamier sauce, mix the cornstarch with 1 tablespoon water. Add to the wine mixture and stir until thickened, about 1 minute.

Decrease the heat as necessary so that the mixture is hot but not simmering. Whisk in the butter, a few cubes at a time. (If the butter is added too quickly, the temperature of the sauce will fall too low and the sauce will break, or curdle. If the sauce temperature is too high, 190°F or above, the sauce will also break, or curdle.) After all the butter is incorporated, adjust the heat to keep the sauce hot without simmering; the sauce may be held for up to 2 hours if kept over very low heat.

Season the tilapia lightly with salt and pepper. Place a large skillet over high heat and add the remaining 2 tablespoons olive oil. When the oil is shimmering, add the fish and cover the pan. Cook until the fish loses its transparency, about 3 minutes. Divide the fillets among 6 warm plates and ladle about ¼ cup sauce on top of each. Any remaining sauce can be passed around the table.

Wine pairing A white Côtes du Rhône is the perfect accompaniment for a mild, white fish like tilapia.

Vegetarian

Mushroom Stacks

CELINA TIO

This impressive dish—layers of baked phyllo interspersed with sautéed mushrooms, a panko-crumbed fried egg, and herbed ricotta—can be served for lunch, brunch, or dinner. The ricotta itself can be spread on crostini and served with cocktails or wine.

SERVES 4

PASTRY

3 (9 by 12-inch) sheets phyllo dough, or enough
    sheets to yield 12 (3-inch) squares
2 tablespoons butter, melted
Kosher salt and freshly ground black pepper

MUSHROOMS

1 tablespoon extra virgin olive oil
1½ pounds assorted mushrooms, sliced
1 clove garlic, minced
1 shallot, finely diced
Kosher salt and freshly ground black pepper
2 teaspoons red wine vinegar
¼ cup vegetable stock
1 tablespoon cold butter
1 teaspoon finely sliced fresh chives

1 cup panko (Japanese bread crumbs)
4 large eggs
4 ounces herbed ricotta cheese (page 117)
Chervil sprigs, for garnish
Fruity extra virgin olive oil, or truffle oil,
    for garnish

BAKE THE PHYLLO: Preheat the oven to 375°F. Stack the phyllo sheets on a work surface and cover with a damp towel to avoid drying. Take off one sheet and brush with melted butter. Top with another sheet, brush with butter, and season with a little salt and pepper. Top with one last layer of phyllo and brush with butter. Cut the layered phyllo into 3-inch squares.

Line a baking sheet with parchment paper or a nonstick liner. Place the squares on the sheet, about 2 inches apart. Top with parchment paper or another nonstick liner, and weight the phyllo down with another baking sheet. Bake for 5 minutes, then remove the top baking sheet and parchment, and continue baking until the pastry is golden brown, about 2 more minutes. While they are in the oven, prepare the mushrooms.

MAKE THE MUSHROOMS: Heat the olive oil in a sauté pan over high heat. Add the mushrooms and sauté for 30 seconds. Add the minced garlic and shallot. Season with salt and pepper to taste. Continue to cook for another minute.

Add the vinegar and vegetable stock, and simmer until slightly reduced. Swirl in the cold butter until it is incorporated. Add the chives and adjust with salt and pepper as needed.

Lightly cover the bottom of a large sauté pan with some of the panko. Heat over medium-high heat. Crack the eggs on top of the panko, keeping the eggs from touching one another and the yolks intact. Season with salt and pepper and sprinkle with the remaining panko. Flip each egg, one at a time, after 30 seconds; the eggs should be cooked over easy. Remove the eggs from the pan and cut around each yolk so that the over easy eggs are the same size and shape as the phyllo squares.

TO SERVE: Place 1 egg in the center of each of 4 serving plates. Top with 1 to 2 tablespoons ricotta, then a phyllo square. Add a serving of mushrooms and another square of phyllo. Garnish with chervil and drizzle with olive oil or truffle oil.

Wine pairing Egg yolks have a tendency to coat the palate and obscure the taste of a good wine. To overcome this, serve a crisp, sparkling white wine from Alsace or a sparkling Cava from Spain.

Pasta with Heirloom Tomatoes, Fresh Mozzarella, Basil, and Balsamic Vinaigrette

NORA POUILLON

Restaurant Nora, in Washington, D.C., was the first certified organic restaurant in the country. A simple pasta dish like this is all about the ingredients, so use the best tomatoes, mozzarella, and herbs you can find. This is a wonderful example of healthy and organic food at its delicious best.

SERVES 4

BALSAMIC VINAIGRETTE

1½ tablespoons balsamic vinegar

¼ teaspoon sea salt

½ teaspoon minced garlic

3½ tablespoons extra virgin olive oil

Freshly ground black pepper

3 to 4 pounds heirloom tomatoes, cored and
    cut into ¾-inch dice

1 cup fresh basil, finely julienned

½ pound fresh mozzarella, cut into ½-inch cubes

Salt

1 pound fresh or dried fettuccine, spaghetti,
    or penne

1 teaspoon extra virgin olive oil

Basil leaves, for garnish (optional)

Combine the balsamic vinegar, salt, and garlic in a small bowl. Slowly whisk in the olive oil. Season with pepper and additional salt as needed.

Toss the tomatoes with the balsamic vinaigrette, julienned basil leaves, and mozzarella in a medium bowl; set the tomato salad aside.

Bring a large pot of lightly salted water to a boil. Add the pasta and boil until al dente. Drain in a colander and toss with the olive oil.

Pour the pasta into a large, warmed serving bowl, top with the tomato salad, and toss to mix. Garnish with basil leaves, and serve. Alternatively, divide the pasta among 4 large, warmed soup plates and arrange several spoonfuls of the tomato salad on top. Garnish with basil leaves and serve.

Wine pairing Seasonal heirloom tomatoes make this dish and they deserve a wine that showcases them. A medium-bodied, fruity Tuscan Sangiovese fits that bill. A lightly chilled Rosato would also be a refreshing choice.

Pasta Primavera

SIRIO MACCIONI

Pasta primavera—spaghetti with bright springtime vegetables—is one of the most-copied recipes to ever come out of a restaurant. The secret to Sirio Maccioni's unrivaled recipe is the mascarpone, which makes the sauce smooth and adds a slightly tangy flavor to the sweet tomatoes.

SERVES 2 AS A MAIN COURSE,
OR 4 AS A FIRST COURSE

Salt

4 tablespoons extra virgin olive oil

¾ cup heavy cream

3 tablespoons mascarpone cheese

1 tablespoon unsalted butter

½ cup grated Parmigiano-Reggiano cheese,
    or as needed

Freshly ground black pepper

½ cup pine nuts

1 cup thinly sliced white mushrooms

About ½ medium zucchini, quartered lengthwise
    and sliced ¼ inch thick (1 cup)

1 cup broccoli florets

½ cup fresh or defrosted frozen peas

1 tablespoon finely chopped garlic

3 sprigs basil leaves, finely chopped

1 cup coarsely chopped fresh or canned plum
    tomatoes

½ pound spaghettini

2 tablespoons finely chopped Italian parsley

In a large pot, bring 1 gallon of water, 1 tablespoon of salt, and 1 tablespoon of the olive oil to a boil. Decrease the heat to a low simmer until ready to cook the pasta.

Combine the cream, mascarpone cheese, butter, and ½ cup of the Parmesan in a small saucepan over low heat. Simmer until the sauce is lightly thickened, about 5 minutes. Season with salt and pepper. Set aside, keeping the sauce warm.

Heat 2 tablespoons of the olive oil in a small skillet over high heat. Add the pine nuts and toss until they are a very light brown. Watch the nuts carefully so they don't burn. Add the mushrooms, zucchini, broccoli, and fresh peas. Toss well until crisp-tender, 5 to 7 minutes. If using defrosted frozen peas, add in the last 2 minutes of cooking. Season with salt and pepper. Set aside, keeping warm.

Heat the remaining 1 tablespoon olive oil in a small skillet over medium heat. Add the garlic and basil and sauté until the garlic is softened but not browned, about 2 minutes. Add the tomatoes, decrease the heat to low, and sauté for another 3 to 4 minutes.

Bring the water in the pasta pot back to a boil and add the spaghettini. Stir and cook until just al dente. Drain and return the pasta to the pot. Add the Parmesan cream sauce, sautéed vegetables, tomatoes, and chopped parsley. Toss well and adjust the salt, pepper, and Parmesan.

Wine pairing *A medium-bodied red wine with cherry notes, such as the Montepulciano/ Sangiovese blends from the Marches region of Italy, beautifully handles the nutty Parmigiano and fresh vegetables.*

Vegetable Pot-au-Feu

PILAR SANCHEZ

Pot-au-feu is a hearty, traditional French dish of various meats and vegetables simmered in water. It resembles an Italian bollito misto or a New England boiled dinner, the difference being the kinds of meats used in each one. This vegetarian meal-in-a-pot deserves some crusty rustic bread for soaking up the broth.

SERVES 4 TO 6

8 cups vegetable or chicken stock

1 (2-inch) piece Parmigiano-Reggiano cheese
    rind

½ pound baby beets (Chioggia beets with
    their striated colors are nice)

½ pound baby carrots

½ pound baby zucchini

½ pound baby summer squash

¼ pound (about ¾ cup after removed from pods)
    fava beans (fresh or frozen) or edamame

¼ pound shelled peas

Kosher salt and ground white pepper

Chervil or Italian parsley sprigs, for garnish

Extra virgin olive oil, for garnish

Combine the stock with the cheese rind in a large saucepan over medium-low heat. Partially cover and simmer for about 1 hour.

Meanwhile, preheat the oven to 375°F. Wrap the beets in aluminum foil, crimp the edges of the packet to seal, and place on a baking sheet. Roast until tender when pierced with a knife, about 45 minutes. When cool enough to handle, remove the foil and rub off the skins. Set the beets aside.

To blanch the vegetables, bring a large pot of water to a boil. Prepare a large bowl of ice water. Add the carrots to the boiling water, and allow to boil until they are crisp-tender, 1 to 2 minutes. Quickly immerse them in the ice water, about 10 seconds, then remove, drain, and set aside. Add the zucchini and squash to the boiling water and allow them to boil just until they turn bright green and yellow, about 30 seconds. Quickly immerse them in the ice water, about 10 seconds, then remove, drain, and set aside. Add the fava beans to the water and allow them to boil for 20 seconds. Remove with a slotted spoon and rinse under cold water. Drain and peel to remove the translucent skin from each bean. Set aside. Add the peas to the boiling water, and allow them to boil for 10 seconds. Quickly immerse them in the ice water, then remove, drain, and set aside.

Remove and discard the cheese rind from the pot of broth. Add the beets, carrots, zucchini, squash, fava beans, and peas. Bring to a boil, and then remove from the heat. Season with salt and pepper to taste. Ladle the broth and vegetables into warm bowls or soup plates, and garnish with chervil and a few drops of olive oil.

Wine pairing With so many flavors and vegetables at play in this winter stew, a light- to medium-bodied red, such as a Chinon from the Loire Valley, is able to bring it all together.

Wild Mushroom Lasagna

DAPHNE ARAUJO

Vintner Daphne Araujo of Araujo Estate Wines adapted this recipe from her friend, chef Susan Costner. Daphne, a landscape architect by trade, is known in the Valley for her unique style and warm hospitality. Along with their highly prized Cabernet Sauvignon, Syrah, and Sauvignon Blanc wines, the Araujos also produce olive oil and honey. This lasagna is a bit more sophisticated than the usual version. For a larger crowd, double the recipe.

SERVES 6

MUSHROOMS AND PASTA

2 cups water

1 ounce dried porcini mushrooms

2 dry-packed sun-dried tomato halves

3 tablespoons olive oil

2 tablespoons unsalted butter

2 pounds assorted fresh mixed mushrooms, halved or quartered, or sliced if large

1 medium onion, finely chopped

1 tablespoon chopped fresh thyme

2 cloves garlic, finely chopped

1 cup red wine

1 (14-ounce) can Italian plum tomatoes with juices

¼ cup chopped Italian parsley

Salt and freshly ground black pepper

1 (1-pound) box lasagna noodles

BÉCHAMEL SAUCE

½ cup (1 stick) butter

3 tablespoons all-purpose flour

2 cups milk

Freshly grated nutmeg

Salt

⅓ cup freshly grated Parmigiano-Reggiano cheese

1 tablespoon unsalted butter, cut into tiny cubes

FOR THE MUSHROOMS AND PASTA: Bring the water to a boil and pour over the dried mushrooms and sun-dried tomatoes. Let sit for 15 minutes. Reserving the liquid, remove the mushrooms and tomatoes and rinse under running water. Squeeze dry, coarsely chop, and reserve. Strain the reserved liquid though a fine-meshed sieve or cheesecloth and set aside.

Heat 2 tablespoons of the olive oil and the butter in a large skillet over medium heat. Add the fresh mushrooms, increase the heat to medium-high, and sauté until all the liquid has been released and evaporated and the mushrooms are nicely browned. Transfer the mushrooms to a plate and wipe the pan clean. Add the remaining 1 tablespoon olive oil, the onion, and the thyme. Cover and cook over medium-low heat until the onion is softened but not browned, about 5 minutes. Uncover, add the garlic, and stir until the onion is just beginning to brown.

Add the wine and reserved liquid from the dried mushrooms and sun-dried tomatoes. Simmer until the liquid is reduced by half. Add the canned tomatoes and their juices, parsley, fresh mushroom mixture, and the chopped dried mushrooms and sun-dried tomatoes. Bring to a simmer and cook, uncovered, until most of the liquid has evaporated, about 15 minutes. Season with salt and pepper to taste. Remove from the heat and set aside.

Bring a large pot of lightly salted water to a boil. Add the lasagna noodles one at a time (to prevent sticking) and cook until just al dente, about 6 minutes; *do not overcook*. Drain and rinse each noodle under cold running water and lay out on clean tea towels to drain.

MAKE THE BÉCHAMEL SAUCE: In a small saucepan over low heat, melt the butter. Add the flour, whisking to prevent lumps, and cook for 2 to 3 minutes. Whisk in the milk and increase the heat to medium. Continue to whisk until smooth and thickened, about 8 minutes. Add the nutmeg and season with salt to taste. Remove from the heat and set aside.

Preheat the oven to 425°F. Brush or spray an 8 by 10-inch baking pan with olive oil. Carefully line the bottom of the pan with one layer of slightly overlapping noodles. Spread one-third of the vegetable mixture over the noodles, and then cover with one-quarter of the béchamel and 1 tablespoon of the Parmesan cheese. Repeat this layering two more times. Top with a final layer of noodles, and cover with the remaining béchamel and cheese. Dot the top of the lasagna with the butter. (If desired, cover and refrigerate for up to 8 hours before baking; bring to room temperature before placing in the oven.)

Bake until lightly browned on top and heated through, about 25 minutes. To see if it is heated through, insert the tip of a knife into the center of the lasagna; if the knife is hot when it comes out, the lasagna is ready. Allow to stand for 10 minutes before serving.

Wine pairing Daphne sent her own wine selection with this recipe—she likes to serve a Brunello di Montalcino from Tuscany with this hearty, full-flavored dish.

Meat

Beef Tenderloin with Soy-Glazed Mushrooms

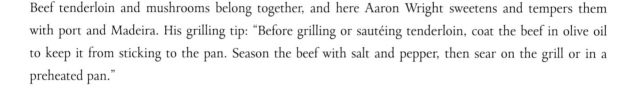

AARON WRIGHT

Beef tenderloin and mushrooms belong together, and here Aaron Wright sweetens and tempers them with port and Madeira. His grilling tip: "Before grilling or sautéing tenderloin, coat the beef in olive oil to keep it from sticking to the pan. Season the beef with salt and pepper, then sear on the grill or in a preheated pan."

SERVES 4

PORT REDUCTION

1 (750-milliliter) bottle ruby port

MUSHROOMS

¼ cup extra virgin olive oil

1 pound cremini mushrooms

2 shallots, sliced

¼ cup light soy sauce

¾ cup Madeira

Salt and freshly ground black pepper

2 tablespoons unsalted butter

BEEF

4 (6-ounce) beef tenderloin fillets

Extra virgin olive oil

Salt and freshly ground black pepper

Mixed baby greens, for serving

Sliced scallions, for serving

Extra virgin olive oil

MAKE THE PORT REDUCTION: In a large saucepan over medium-high heat, reduce the port to a glaze. When the volume is reduced to about three-quarters of the original and the surface has a lot of shiny bubbles, the glaze is nearly finished. Decrease the heat to medium and continue to simmer for a few more minutes. Check the consistency by looking for a steady stream to come off the spoon when pouring. When the reduction pours in a continuous unbroken line, turn off the heat and let the mixture cool to room temperature. (The reduction may be refrigerated for up to 1 month. Chilling will gel the reduction; allow it to warm to room temperature before serving.)

MAKE THE MUSHROOMS: Heat the olive oil in a large sauté pan over medium heat. Add the mushrooms and shallots and sauté until lightly browned. Add the soy sauce and Madeira, bring to a boil, and reduce the liquid. Season with salt and pepper to taste. When most of the liquid has evaporated, add the butter to the pan and remove from the heat. Cover and keep warm until serving.

GRILL THE BEEF: Preheat a large sauté pan or grill over high heat. Brush all sides of the fillets with a thin layer of olive oil and season generously with salt and pepper. Sauté or grill to the desired doneness (the internal temperature will read 130 to 140°F for medium-rare).

Mix the greens and scallions in a large bowl. Toss with olive oil, salt, and pepper. Spoon the mushrooms into the center of each of 4 plates. Drizzle some of the port reduction around the mushrooms. Place a portion of the greens on top of the mushrooms, and top the greens with a tenderloin. Serve immediately.

Wine pairing A New World-style Pinot Noir with bright red fruit flavors and a trace of Asian spice will add the needed balance between the tangy soy and the sweet Madeira.

Braised Short Ribs

SCOTT BRYAN

No other dish goes as well with the heartiest of red wines as braised short ribs. Rich and deeply flavored from a long, slow braise, these ribs are served with gravy on a bed of polenta or whipped potatoes and pan-roasted root vegetables. Scott Bryan created this recipe for the New York restaurant Veritas, where owner Park Smith's wine list of more than 100,000 bottles guarantees plenty of choices for matching these short ribs.

SERVES 4

4 plum tomatoes

4 pounds short ribs

Salt and freshly ground black pepper

6 tablespoons butter

1 large head garlic, cloves separated and peeled

2 (750-milliliter) bottles light, fruity red wine, such as Dolcetto

6 sprigs rosemary

2 sprigs thyme

2 sprigs sage

1 cup diced onion

1 cup diced carrot

1 cup diced celery

½ pound porcini mushrooms, sliced

4 tablespoons sliced chives, for garnish

Preheat the oven to 350°F. Bring a medium pot of water to a boil. Drop in the tomatoes for 10 to 15 seconds to loosen the skins. Remove the tomatoes with a wire skimmer and rinse under cold running water. Gently slit the skins and peel them off. Halve the tomatoes, squeeze to remove the seeds, and dice the pulp; set aside. Season the short ribs liberally with salt and pepper.

Place a Dutch oven over high heat and allow to sit for 1 minute. Melt 2 tablespoons of the butter in the pot and immediately add the ribs, searing them until well browned, 4 to 5 minutes on each side. Transfer the ribs to a plate.

Return the Dutch oven to the stovetop, decrease the heat to low, add the garlic and tomatoes, and cook until soft. Add the wine and bring to a boil. Add the ribs and baste with the wine and vegetables. Add 2 of the rosemary sprigs and the thyme and sage sprigs. Cover, place in the oven, and braise for 2½ hours, or until the ribs are tender.

Remove the ribs from the pot. Strain the cooking juices though a fine-meshed strainer, and discard the solids. Return the ribs to the pot and pour the sauce over the ribs.

Melt 2 tablespoons of the butter in a large skillet over medium heat. Add the onion, carrot, and celery. Cover and cook, stirring once or twice, until the vegetables are tender and pale, 2 to 3 minutes; do not allow them to brown. Add the vegetables to the ribs.

Heat the remaining 2 tablespoons butter in a small pan. Add the mushrooms and sauté, stirring frequently, until golden. Add the mushrooms to the ribs. Season with salt and pepper to taste. To serve, gently spoon the ribs, sauce, and vegetables onto serving plates and garnish with the chives and remaining 4 rosemary sprigs.

Wine pairing This robust dish relies on the integrated flavors that only result from patient preparation. The wine selection deserves the same thoughtfulness. Either a Chianti Classico from Tuscany or a Rioja Reserva from Spain would make a worthy companion.

Calf's Liver and Onions

CHRIS BENNETT

Chris Bennett has recently reinvented Doug Arango's into the Melrose Bar and Grill in West Hollywood. No one makes calf's liver better than he does. I absolutely love the way he prepares it—infused with rosemary, lots of black pepper, and paper-thin onions. His side of choice is old-fashioned mashed potatoes.

SERVES 2

½ cup extra virgin olive oil

2 medium onions, thinly sliced

2 slices bacon

6 sprigs rosemary

2 (6-ounce) thin slices calf's liver

Salt and freshly ground black pepper

All-purpose flour, for dredging

2 tablespoons sherry vinegar

1 teaspoon Worcestershire sauce

¼ cup chicken stock

1 tablespoon unsalted butter, at room
    temperature

Heat the olive oil in a large sauté pan over medium-high heat. When the oil is shimmering, add the onions, bacon, and rosemary. Cook, adjusting the heat as necessary, until the bacon is crispy and the onions are a rich golden brown. Remove the bacon with tongs when browned, transferring to a paper towel to drain. When the onions have browned, transfer to paper towels and discard the rosemary. Set aside the pan, leaving the bacon fat in it. Season the livers with salt and pepper. Dredge in flour, shaking off any excess.

Return the sauté pan with the reserved fat to the stovetop, and increase the heat to high. When the pan is hot, sauté the livers until crispy, 30 to 45 seconds on each side for medium. Transfer the cooked livers to warmed dinner plates.

Carefully discard the hot oil and return the pan to the heat. Add the vinegar and Worcestershire sauce and reduce slightly. Add the stock, butter, salt, and pepper. Simmer until the sauce is thick and reduced by about one-half. Spoon the sauce over the liver, top with the onions and bacon, and serve.

Wine pairing A medium-bodied, fruity Zinfandel brings out the sweetness of the onions and cuts the richness of the liver and bacon.

Côte de Chevreuil
(Pan-Roasted Venison with Red Wine–Braised Cabbage and Sauce Poivrade)

THOMAS KELLER

The dishes served at Thomas Keller's restaurants—French Laundry, in Yountville, California, and New York's Per Se—are known for their attention to every detail, including ingredients, preparation, and presentation. Create a bit of Keller's magic by preparing this game entrée in your own kitchen.

SERVES 6

CABBAGE

2 heads red cabbage, quartered, cored,
    and sliced ⅛ inch thick

⅔ cup port

⅔ cup red wine

2 slices bacon

2 Spanish onions

1 cup honey

½ cup red wine vinegar

4 Granny Smith apples, peeled, cored, and grated

2 potatoes, peeled and grated

Kosher salt and freshly ground black pepper

VENISON

⅓ cup grapeseed oil

1 (2½-pound) rack of venison

Kosher salt and freshly ground black pepper

1 bunch thyme

SAUCE POIVRADE

⅓ cup grapeseed oil

1 pound venison bones, cut into 1-inch pieces

1 cup water

1 cup chicken stock

1 cup fresh huckleberries (Sources, see page 164)

2 tablespoons red wine vinegar

3 cups veal or beef stock

1 tablespoon Tellicherry peppercorns, crushed

6 sprigs chervil, for garnish

PREPARE THE CABBAGE: In a large bowl, combine the cabbage, port, and red wine. Marinate overnight.

The next day, preheat the oven to 350°F. Place a large casserole over medium heat, and cook the bacon. When it begins to render, add the onions and cook until wilted. Add the cabbage, honey, and vinegar. Cover with a parchment paper lid. Bake until all the liquid has evaporated, about 1 hour. Mix the apples and potatoes into the cabbage and place the casserole back in the oven for another 30 minutes. Remove from the oven, and season with salt and pepper to taste.

MAKE THE VENISON: In a large sauté pan, heat the grapeseed oil. Season the venison generously with salt and pepper. Place the venison in the pan and evenly brown all sides for about 1 minute each. Remove from the pan, and reserve until the cabbage is almost ready. To finish the venison, place in a sauté pan over medium heat, add the thyme, and cook until medium-rare, 12 to 18 minutes. Remove and let rest before carving.

FOR THE SAUCE POIVRADE: Heat the oil over medium heat in a heavy stockpot and add the venison bones. Cook until well browned. Add the water and reduce, stirring, until the liquid begins to glaze the bottom of the pan. Deglaze the chicken stock and reduce again. Add the huckleberries and vinegar, and reduce until dry. Add the veal stock, reduce by one-half, and strain. Add the peppercorns and continue cooking until you are left with about 1 cup of sauce that coats the back of a spoon.

To serve, place about 2 tablespoons sauce in the center of each of 6 plates. Spoon some cabbage on top of the sauce, then place 2 pieces of venison on top of the cabbage, slightly overlapping each other. Garnish with a sprig of chervil and two turns of a pepper mill on the side of the plate.

Wine pairing The distinct game flavor of the venison coupled with the jammy huckleberry is well suited for a New World fruit-forward Australian Grenache.

Fresh Stracci Pasta with Ragú Bolognese

JAMES FIALA

Jimmy's casual restaurant, Acero, is dedicated to the Italian home cooking he learned from his mother. *Stracci* means "rags" in Italian, so if making your own pasta, roll the dough out thinly and then cut it into irregular pieces about 1 by 3 inches. Dried bucatini, rigatoni, or penne rigate can be substituted.

SERVES 6

PASTA

2 ¾ cups semolina flour

5 large eggs

RAGÚ BOLOGNESE

3 carrots, finely chopped

2 small onions

3 stalks celery, finely chopped

6 cloves garlic, finely chopped

1 tablespoon extra virgin olive oil, plus
   additional for drizzling

1 ½ pounds ground beef

Salt

1 (750-milliliter) bottle dry red wine

2 large tomatoes, peeled, seeded, quartered
   (or a 12-ounce can of peeled tomatoes)

1 (6-ounce) can tomato paste

2 bay leaves

1 cup heavy cream

Freshly ground black pepper

2 to 3 tablespoons freshly grated Parmigiano-
   Reggiano cheese

4 fresh basil leaves, torn

MAKE THE PASTA DOUGH: Place the semolina on a work surface and make a well in the center. Crack the eggs into the well and whip the egg mixture with a fork until half of the semolina is incorporated. Knead the rest of the semolina into the dough until it is completely incorporated. If the dough is dry, add a few teaspoons of water. Wrap the dough in plastic wrap and refrigerate for at least 2 hours and up to 1 day.

PREPARE THE RAGÚ: Using a food processor, finely chop the carrots, onions, celery, and garlic. Place a wide heavy pot over high heat. When the pot is hot, add the olive oil, ground beef, and a few pinches of salt. When the beef is brown, spoon or drain off any excess fat. Add the chopped vegetables and cook, stirring frequently, for 5 minutes. Add the red wine, tomatoes, tomato paste, and bay leaves. Lower the heat and simmer until reduced to a chili-like thickness, about 40 minutes. While the ragú is cooking, roll and cut the pasta.

ROLL AND CUT THE PASTA: Cut the dough into balls about 2 inches in diameter, and roll out into long oval shapes about ⅛-inch thick. Cut the pasta crosswise every 4 inches. Cut each 4-inch piece crosswise again (perpendicular to the first cuts) to form 3 by 1-inch rectangles.

When the ragú is reduced, add the cream and season with salt and pepper. Return heat to a low simmer.

Place a large pot of lightly salted water over high heat and bring to a boil. Add the stracci to the boiling water, cook for about 45 seconds, and drain. Add the pasta to the ragú and stir to mix. Top each serving with grated Parmesan, chopped fresh basil, and a drizzle of olive oil.

Wine pairing Pasta sauce with big flavors calls for a big wine. The Maremma region of Tuscany's coast produces wine based on Sangiovese with the New World twists that meld Cabernet Sauvignon and Merlot into the mix. Or, how about a full-blown Aglianico from Campania?

Peppered Beef Tenderloin with Shiitake, Cabernet, and Toasted Garlic Sauce with Whipped Yukon Gold Potatoes

LOU ROOK III

Annie Gunn's and its specialty food store, the Smokehouse Market, are must-visit destinations in the Chesterfield Valley west of St. Louis. At the restaurant, Chef Lou Rook prepares his shiitake-cabernet steak sauce with veal stock. And what better side than buttery, whipped potatoes?

SERVES 2

BEEF TENDERLOIN

2 (10-ounce) center-cut beef tenderloins

Extra virgin olive oil

1 tablespoon kosher salt

3 tablespoons freshly cracked black pepper

MUSHROOM SAUCE

2 tablespoons extra virgin olive oil

½ pound shiitake or morel mushrooms, or any combination of fresh mushrooms

2 cloves garlic, minced

6 tablespoons Cabernet Sauvignon

6 tablespoons brown veal or beef stock

1 tablespoon fresh thyme

2 tablespoons unsalted butter

Kosher salt

Cracked black peppercorns

WHIPPED YUKON GOLD POTATOES

1 pound Yukon gold potatoes, peeled

1 cup heavy cream

4 tablespoons (½ stick) unsalted butter, at room temperature

Kosher salt

Ground white pepper

PREPARE THE BEEF: Preheat the grill. Massage the beef fillets with the olive oil. Combine the salt and cracked pepper on a flat plate and roll the fillets to coat. Sear the tenderloins on the grill for about 3 minutes on each side (turning once), or until an instant-read thermometer inserted into the center of the meat reads 120 to 130°F. For medium-rare, cook 4 minutes per side (130 to 135°F), and for medium, cook 5 to 6 minutes per side (140 to 145°F).

MAKE THE MUSHROOM SAUCE: Place a large skillet over medium heat and add the oil. When the oil is hot, add the mushrooms and sauté until they give up their juices and then reabsorb them. Add the garlic and allow to brown slightly. Add the wine and stir with a wooden spoon, scraping the bottom of the pan, until the wine is reduced to one-quarter its original volume. Add the stock and reduce by one-half. Add the thyme, butter, salt, and cracked pepper to taste. Keep warm until ready to serve.

MAKE THE POTATOES: Place the potatoes in a pot with water to cover, and bring to a boil. Lower to a simmer and skim the foam off the top. Cook until tender. Meanwhile, combine the cream and butter in a small saucepan, and heat just until the butter is melted and the cream is steaming; do not boil.

Drain the cooked potatoes. Return them to the pot and press through a sieve or force them through a ricer. Add the warm butter and cream mixture. Season with kosher salt and white pepper. Whip the potatoes vigorously with a potato masher, or use a handheld mixer on the low setting, being careful not to beat too long.

To serve, place a fillet on each plate and top with mushroom sauce and mashed potatoes.

Wine pairing Tenderloin is a classic beef entrée. For the ultimate experience, open and decant a rich, full-bodied Cabernet Sauvignon from the Napa Valley or a renowned Bordeaux.

Grilled Rib-Eye with Bone Marrow Bread Pudding, Fiddlehead Ferns, and Chimichurri Sauce

KEVIN NASHAN

Kevin Nashan is chef/owner of the Sidney Street Cafe, located in a beautifully restored neighborhood of St. Louis known as Soulard, where one of the country's oldest farmers' markets still exists. I still shop there, as did my mother, grandmother, and great-grandmother. Kevin and his wife, Mina, have created a unique menu full of showstoppers like this grilled rib-eye sensation. Call your butcher in advance for the bone marrow so you'll be sure to have it when you need it.

SERVES 6

CHIMICHURRI SAUCE

1 cup (packed) Italian parsley

8 to 10 cloves garlic, minced

1 cup extra virgin olive oil

3 tablespoons freshly squeezed lemon juice

1 teaspoon hot red pepper flakes

1 teaspoon granulated sugar

Salt

6 (12-ounce) rib-eye steaks

BREAD PUDDING

½ pound uncooked veal or beef bone marrow
    (or combination of both)

3 teaspoons salt

Freshly ground black pepper

1 to 1¼ pounds (about 3 loaves) brioche, crusts
    removed and cut into 1-inch cubes

2 cups heavy cream

4 sprigs thyme

1 bay leaf

¼ cup brown sugar

8 large egg yolks

1½ pounds fiddlehead ferns, trimmed

2 tablespoons butter

5 tablespoons freshly grated Parmigiano-
    Reggiano cheese

MAKE THE CHIMICHURRI SAUCE: Fill a medium saucepan with lightly salted water, and place over high heat to bring to a boil. Meanwhile, set aside a bowl of ice water. Blanch the parsley in the boiling water for 5 seconds, then drain and plunge into the ice water. Drain again and squeeze dry.

Combine the parsley and garlic in a food processor and pulse until puréed. With the machine running, drizzle in the olive oil and lemon juice. Add the red pepper flakes, sugar, and salt to taste, pulsing to mix. Place half of the sauce in a covered container, and refrigerate until needed. Bring to room temperature before serving. Spread the remaining half of the sauce in a wide shallow dish or pan large enough to hold the steaks in one layer.

Place the steaks in the dish with the chimichurri sauce, and turn to coat them well on all sides. Set aside at room temperature.

MAKE THE BREAD PUDDING: Season the bone marrow with 1 teaspoon of the salt and some pepper. Place a skillet over medium heat, and add the marrow, turning to brown it evenly on all sides. Remove the marrow from the pan, reserving the fat in the pan, and cut into ½-inch dice; set aside.

Preheat the oven to 425°F. Oil an 8-inch square baking pan (or other small baking pan) with some of the reserved bone marrow fat. Pour the rest of the fat into a mixing bowl, and add the bone marrow and diced brioche.

In a 2-quart saucepan, combine the cream, thyme, bay leaf, brown sugar, and the remaining 2 teaspoons of salt. Place over medium-low heat and bring to a simmer, then remove from the heat.

Place the egg yolks in a mixing bowl and whisk until blended. Vigorously whisk the cream mixture in the saucepan while you add about ½ cup of the yolks into the mixture. Whisk the remaining yolks vigorously, then slowly blend the cream mixture into the yolks.

Drizzle the cream mixture into the bowl of bone marrow and brioche, using just enough to coat the bread. Toss gently and transfer to the baking pan, spreading it evenly. Pour the remaining cream evenly over the top. Bake until a toothpick inserted into the middle comes out clean, about 30 minutes.

MAKE THE FIDDLEHEAD FERNS: Fill a large stockpot with lightly salted water, and bring to a boil. Set aside a large bowl filled with ice water. Add the fiddlehead ferns to the boiling water and cook just until they are bright green and barely tender, 1 to 2 minutes. Drain and immediately plunge into the ice water. Drain again, and set aside.

Preheat a gas grill to 450°F or prepare a hot fire in a charcoal grill. Season the marinated steaks with salt and pepper, and grill as desired, about 135°F in the center for medium-rare steaks.

Melt the butter in a skillet, add the fiddlehead ferns, and sauté until tender, 1 to 2 minutes. Transfer to a warm serving bowl. Toss with the Parmesan to combine. Set aside, keeping warm.

To serve, place a steak on each of 6 large plates, and add a portion of bone marrow pudding and fiddlehead ferns. Drizzle a small spoonful of the reserved chimichurri sauce on each steak, and pass the remainder separately.

Wine pairing Barolo is one of the Nebbiolo-based wines known for their "tar and roses" flavor. They are ideal reds for grilled meats. Barolo is especially nice in the way it mirrors the smokiness of grilled meat.

Grilled Pork Tenderloin with Roasted Vegetables and Truffle Risotto

MICHAEL ROZZI

Michael Rozzi's Della Femina is a Hamptons destination, and this is one of his favorite recipes from the restaurant. Marinated with rosemary and juniper, then grilled, this pork tenderloin is served on a bed of risotto, surrounded by caramelized roasted vegetables. When friends offer to help, take them up on it, so one person can tend to the grill, another to the risotto. Chef's note: If fresh truffles are unavailable, substitute canned truffles or garnish with truffle oil.

SERVES 10 TO 12

TENDERLOINS

2 tablespoons juniper berries

1 tablespoon coarsely chopped fresh rosemary

1 tablespoon chopped garlic

1 tablespoon sweet Spanish paprika (pimentón)

1 teaspoon cracked black peppercorns

1 cup canola oil

3 pounds pork tenderloins, trimmed of fat

VEGETABLES

12 baby red beets or 6 small beets,
   halved or quartered

12 baby gold beets or 6 small beets,
   halved or quartered

12 baby turnips or 6 small turnips,
   halved or quartered

24 (2-inch) baby carrots

Extra virgin olive oil

Salt and freshly ground black pepper

RISOTTO

4 cups chicken or vegetable broth

3 tablespoons extra virgin olive oil

2 tablespoons unsalted butter

1 medium onion, finely diced

2½ cups Arborio rice

1 bay leaf (preferably fresh)

1 cup dry white wine

¼ cup honey

1 cup freshly grated Parmigiano-Reggiano cheese

3 to 4 ounces black winter truffles (optional)

MARINATE THE PORK: Place a small skillet over medium heat and add the juniper berries. Stir or shake the pan until the berries are toasted and fragrant. Chop the berries and place in a shallow dish large enough to hold the pork. Add the rosemary, garlic, paprika, peppercorns, and canola oil. Add the tenderloins and stir until well coated. Cover and refrigerate for 24 to 48 hours. While the pork is marinating, prepare the vegetables.

MAKE THE VEGETABLES: Preheat the oven to 350°F. Place the red beets and gold beets in a baking dish and roast for 30 minutes, or until tender. Meanwhile, bring lightly salted water to a boil in a medium saucepan. Prepare a bowl of ice water. Add the turnips to the boiling water, simmer just until tender, drain, and cool in the ice water. Remove the skins and put in a bowl with the beets and carrots. Cover and refrigerate for 24 to 48 hours.

Preheat the oven to 350°F. Arrange the beets, carrots, and turnips in a large roasting pan in a single layer. Drizzle and coat the vegetables with olive oil and season with salt and pepper to taste. Roast until the vegetables are caramelized and soft, about 20 minutes. Prepare the risotto while the vegetables are roasting.

MAKE THE RISOTTO: Place the broth in a medium saucepan over medium-low heat and bring to a simmer; keep warm. Place a large saucepan or Dutch oven over medium-high heat and add the oil and butter. Add the onion and sauté until translucent. Add the rice and stir to coat with the butter and oil, about 2 minutes. Add the bay leaf and wine and cook, stirring, until the wine is absorbed. Pour in warm broth until the rice is covered. Bring to a simmer and continue to add broth as it becomes absorbed, 1 cup at a time, stirring often with a wooden spoon. When all or most of the broth is used (it may not all be needed) and the rice is tender, remove from the heat and cover loosely.

Preheat the grill. Drizzle the roasted vegetables with the honey; set aside, keeping warm. Remove the pork from the marinade, pat dry with paper towels, and season with salt and pepper. Grill, turning as needed, until the internal temperature reaches 150°F on a meat thermometer, 7 to 8 minutes per side. Place on a cool area of the grill to rest.

Add the Parmesan to the risotto, and stir to a creamy consistency. Season to taste with salt and pepper. Pour the rice onto a medium platter. Using a truffle slicer, shave the truffles over the top of the risotto. Slice the pork into ½-inch-thick medallions and arrange on top of the risotto. Spoon the vegetables onto the platter and serve.

Wine pairing An elegant Barbaresco and shaved truffles are made for each other. Don't worry about overwhelming the pork—it simply basks in the flavors of the wine.

Grilled Venison Steaks with Mushrooms, Spiced Pumpkin, and Cranberry-Orange Relish

MATT McGUIRE

Pumpkin, mushrooms, and cranberry accompany venison loin steaks in this autumnal dish. Serve at your Thanksgiving dinner in place of or in addition to the traditional turkey. Matt suggests pork loin makes a fine substitute if venison is not available.

SERVES 6

CRANBERRY-ORANGE RELISH

1 cup dried cranberries

1 cup Cointreau or other orange-flavored liqueur

1 vanilla bean

1 cup granulated sugar

1 cup water

1 tablespoon butter

2 shallots, thinly sliced

1 orange, zest finely grated and reserved, pith removed, and flesh cut into sections

2 tablespoons chopped Italian parsley

1 tablespoon chopped fresh basil

Salt and freshly ground black pepper

SPICED PUMPKIN

1 cup (2 sticks) butter

2 medium yellow onions, sliced

Salt and freshly ground black pepper

1 (3½- to 4-pound) pumpkin, cored, peeled, seeded, and chopped

¼ cup sherry vinegar

½ cup brown sugar

4 cups chicken stock

2 tablespoons Szechuan peppercorns, finely ground in a spice grinder or with a mortar and pestle

VEGETABLES AND VENISON

½ cup (1 stick) unsalted butter

3 parsnips, diced

¼ cup honey

Salt and freshly ground black pepper

1 cup pearl onions, peeled

4 medium portobello mushrooms, gills scraped off, diced

¼ cup sherry vinegar

6 (6-ounce) venison loin steaks

PREPARE THE RELISH: Place the cranberries in a small heatproof bowl. In a small saucepan over high heat, bring the Cointreau to a vigorous boil. Using a long match, carefully light the Cointreau and allow the flames to burn out. Pour the liqueur over the dried cranberries, and allow them to sit until rehydrated, about 30 minutes. Once they are soft, drain and reserve the cranberries.

Split the vanilla bean lengthwise and scrape the pulp into a medium saucepan. Add the sugar and water. Place over high heat and bring to a simmer, then remove from the heat and reserve.

Melt the butter in a medium saucepan over low heat. Add the shallots and sauté just until translucent. Add the reserved vanilla syrup to the shallots, and simmer for 2 minutes. Pour through a fine-meshed strainer placed over a heatproof bowl and reserve the shallots and syrup separately.

Combine the rehydrated cranberries, orange zest and sections, reserved shallots, parsley, basil, and 2 tablespoons of the vanilla syrup in a medium bowl. Season with salt and pepper to taste. Set aside at room temperature, or cover and refrigerate, warming slightly before serving.

PREPARE THE PUMPKIN: Melt the butter in a large sauté pan or skillet over medium heat. Add the sliced onions and salt and pepper to taste. Cover the pan and cook, stirring once or twice, until the onions are soft and translucent but not browned. Add the pumpkin. Cover and cook until barely tender. Add the vinegar and cook uncovered, stirring, until most of the liquid has evaporated. Add the brown sugar, stock, and Szechuan pepper.

Simmer until the pumpkin is very soft. Purée in a food processor and press through a chinois or fine-meshed strainer. Season with salt and pepper. Set aside, keeping warm, or cover and refrigerate, reheating before serving.

MAKE THE VEGETABLES AND VENISON: Preheat the grill. Place a large sauté pan over medium heat, and melt 4 tablespoons of the butter. Add the parsnips and cook, turning occasionally, until browned and fork-tender in the center, about 20 minutes. Transfer the parsnips to a bowl (reserving the unwashed pan), toss with the honey, and season to taste with salt and pepper. Set aside.

Return the sauté pan to medium heat and add the remaining 4 tablespoons butter. Add the pearl onions and cook, turning occasionally, until lightly golden and just tender, 10 to 15 minutes. Add the mushrooms and sauté until they are tender, about 5 minutes. Add the vinegar and stir with a wooden spoon, scraping the bottom of the pan. Return the parsnips to the pan, and stir to combine. Remove from the heat and keep warm.

Season the venison with salt and pepper. Grill, turning once, about 4 minutes per side for medium-rare steaks. Serve immediately, accompanied by the relish, spiced pumpkin purée, and mixed vegetables.

Wine pairing Malbec, which originated in southwest France, has found a new home in Argentina. These full, rich wines have the structure to support the hearty venison plus a ripe fruitiness for the condiments.

Assyrian Rack of Lamb

NARSAI DAVID

Narsai's Middle Eastern roots are evident in this wonderful lamb dish. The pomegranate-based marinade is his mother's secret recipe. Narsai's note: You will want 1½ lamb racks, which will total about 12 ribs. Ask the butcher to remove the flap of meat, french-cut the rib bones, and cut the chine bone for easy serving.

SERVES 4

1 large onion, coarsely chopped

2 to 3 cloves garlic, peeled

1 teaspoon chopped fresh basil leaves

½ teaspoon salt

½ teaspoon freshly ground black pepper

½ cup pomegranate juice (do not use
    pomegranate syrup)

¼ cup red wine

1½ frenched lamb racks

Wine pairing The elegance of a rack of lamb demands an equally elegant wine. Try a Merlot from the right bank of Bordeaux—either Saint-Émilion or Pomerol. For a domestic wine, Walla Walla in Washington State has some truly sumptuous offerings.

To make the marinade, combine the onion and garlic in a blender or food processor. Process until puréed. Add the basil, salt, pepper, pomegranate juice, and red wine. Process again until smooth.

Place the racks of lamb in a shallow glass or enameled baking dish. Pour the marinade all over the lamb and rub it in well. Cover with plastic wrap and allow to sit at cool room temperature for 6 to 8 hours, or refrigerate overnight. Remove from the refrigerator 1 hour before roasting.

Preheat the oven to 450°F. Wipe off any excess marinade and place the racks in a roasting pan. Roast until an instant-read thermometer inserted into the center of the meat (do not allow it to touch the bone) registers 145°F for medium-rare lamb, 15 to 20 minutes, or as desired.

Slice the racks into chops, arrange on a warm platter, and serve immediately.

Braised Cardamom Beef Stew with Potatoes, Celery Root, and Parsnips

CHARLIE TROTTER

Cardamom, a member of the ginger family, is a staple in Indian and Middle Eastern cuisine. Chef Trotter calls for cardamom pods, but if they are unavailable, 1 teaspoon of ground cardamom can be substituted with similar results. The beef and the vegetables cook separately in the oven, but at the same time, so arrange oven racks accordingly.

SERVES 4

BEEF STEW

2 tablespoons canola oil

1 cup chopped celery

1 cup chopped carrots

2 cups chopped onions

20 cardamom pods, crushed (or 1 teaspoon
    ground cardamom)

2 pounds beef stew meat, cubed

Salt and freshly ground black pepper

1 head garlic, halved

6 cups beef stock

VEGETABLES

3 cups large-diced potatoes

1½ cups large-diced celery root

1½ cups large-diced parsnips

2 to 3 tablespoons extra virgin olive oil

Salt and freshly ground black pepper

MAKE THE STEW: Preheat the oven to 350°F. Place a Dutch oven over medium-high heat. When the pan is hot, add the canola oil, celery, carrots, and onions. Sauté until caramelized, 10 to 15 minutes.

Place the cardamom in a small piece of cheesecloth and tie with kitchen string to form a sachet. Season the beef with salt and pepper and add it to the pan along with the garlic, cardamom sachet, and stock.

Cover the pan and transfer to the oven. Bake until the beef is very tender, 2½ to 3 hours. When the beef is 45 minutes from being done, prepare the vegetables.

ROAST THE VEGETABLES: Toss the potatoes, celery root, and parsnips together with the olive oil in a large bowl. Spread the vegetables evenly on a baking sheet and season with salt and pepper to taste. Roast, tossing occasionally, until the vegetables are golden brown, about 45 minutes.

To serve, place some of the roasted vegetables in the center of each bowl, spoon in the stew, and top with freshly ground black pepper.

Wine pairing A red Saint-Joseph from the northern Rhône has the rich flavors for the root vegetables and a subtle floral bouquet to complement the cardamom.

Poultry

Cavatelli with Braised Duck

RICK TRAMONTO

Rick brings his Italian heritage to the table with a Tuscan-inspired duck ragú. Instead of the traditional pappardelle pasta, he suggests cavatelli to capture all the bits of sauce.

SERVES 4

DUCK AND DUCK SAUCE

2¾ pounds duck legs (3 to 4 legs)

1 pound kosher salt

¾ cup diced carrots

1 onion, cut into large dice

½ stalk celery, cut into large dice

½ cup white mushrooms, halved

1 tablespoon tomato paste

2 tablespoons all-purpose flour

½ (750-milliliter) bottle Cabernet

2 or 3 sprigs thyme

Bay leaf

2 cups veal or beef stock

1 quart chicken stock

STEWED TOMATOES

5 tablespoons extra virgin olive oil

Pinch of hot red pepper flakes

1½ cloves garlic, sliced

2 to 3 sprigs thyme

3 sprigs rosemary

8 whole fresh basil leaves

2½ pounds Roma tomatoes, cored,
    skins lightly scored

Salt

1½ pounds cavatelli

½ cup (1 stick) unsalted butter

4 drops of sherry vinegar

Salt and freshly ground black pepper

About 24 shavings from a wedge of Parmigiano-
    Reggiano cheese

4 basil leaves, minced

PREPARE THE DUCK AND DUCK SAUCE:

Place the duck legs in a large bowl and cover with the kosher salt. Cover and refrigerate for 3 to 5 hours.

Preheat the oven to 300°F. Rinse the salt off the duck legs and pat them dry with paper towels. Place a large braising pan over medium-low heat, and add the duck legs skin-side down. Cover and allow to cook until all the fat is rendered, about 45 minutes. When the legs are fully rendered, reserve ¼ cup of the duck fat, and transfer the legs to a platter. Add the carrots, onion, celery, and mushrooms to the braising pan, and sauté until barely tender and slightly caramelized.

Remove the vegetables from the pan, leaving the fat. Add the tomato paste and flour, and "fry" for 5 minutes, stirring with a whisk. Add the red wine and reduce the sauce by half. Add the duck, vegetables, thyme, and bay leaf, and enough veal stock and chicken stock to cover.

Bring the stock to a boil on top of the stove, then braise the duck until it is tender when pierced with a fork, 2 to 3 hours. Remove the duck from the pan and set aside. Strain the vegetables through a chinois or fine-meshed strainer, pushing all the vegetables and juices into the sauce. Return the sauce to the pan and reduce it by three-quarters. When the duck is cool enough to handle, remove the meat from the bones and add it to the reduced sauce. (If desired, the duck skins may be placed on a baking sheet, dried in the oven until crisp, then coarsely chopped into cracklings for garnish.)

MAKE THE STEWED TOMATOES: Bring a large pot of water to a boil. Meanwhile, in a small saucepan, combine 4 tablespoons of the olive oil, the red pepper flakes, garlic, thyme, rosemary, and basil. Place over low heat to warm and steep the herbs, but do not allow to boil.

Blanch the tomatoes in the boiling water for 7 to 10 seconds. Do not rinse with cold water, but peel when cool enough to handle. Halve the tomatoes lengthwise and squeeze out the juices and seeds. In a large saucepan over medium heat, add the remaining olive oil to the pan. Add the tomatoes and season with salt to taste. Cook until the juices in the pan evaporate. Strain the herbed olive oil into the tomatoes.

FOR ASSEMBLY: Bring a large pot of lightly salted water to a boil, and cook the cavatelli until al dente. Drain the pasta very well.

In large sauté pan or skillet, heat the duck fat until very hot. Add the cavatelli to the pan and cook, stirring frequently, until the pasta turns light brown. Add the duck sauce and quickly reduce by half. Add the butter, vinegar, and stewed tomatoes. Season with salt and pepper to taste. Divide evenly among 4 plates, and garnish with the shaved Parmesan and minced basil.

Wine pairing Northeast Italy offers many fine reds with bright fruit and acidity to balance the rich braised duck. Pour a Lagrein from Trentino or a Valpolicella Ripasso from Veneto to begin this sumptuous meal.

Grilled Chicken Marinated in Rosemary and Olive Oil

TERRANCE BRENNAN

Nothing is more appreciated than a properly grilled chicken. Terrance Brennan's version calls for a cut-up chicken infused with an aromatic rosemary-garlic-lemon marinade. The infused rosemary-garlic oil can also be used on vegetables, fish, or meat. Try his recommendation of Feta-Orzo Salad (page 28) as a salty, tart accompaniment to the chicken.

SERVES 4

⅓ cup extra virgin olive oil

8 cloves garlic, slightly crushed

4 sprigs rosemary

1 lemon, thinly sliced

1 (2- to 3½-pound) chicken, quartered

Feta-Orzo Salad (page 28; optional)

In a small bowl, combine the olive oil, garlic, and rosemary. Squeeze the juice from the lemon into the marinade, then add the rind.

Divide the marinade evenly between 2 heavy-duty gallon-size resealable plastic bags. Place 2 pieces chicken into each bag, seal, and refrigerate for at least 6 hours or overnight.

Preheat a charcoal grill and wait until the coals die down and turn white. Place the chicken pieces on the grill, skin side down, over medium-low heat, and grill until the skin begins to peel, 25 to 30 minutes. Turn the chicken and cook until opaque and white in the center, about 10 more minutes. Test with an instant-read thermometer (160°F for white meat, 170°F for the dark meat or leg).

Allow the chicken to cool to room temperature, then cover and refrigerate until chilled, at least 1 hour. Serve chilled, with the orzo salad.

Wine pairing A zesty Sauvignon Blanc from Sancerre or New Zealand perfectly accompanies the chilled, grilled chicken and vegetables. Sauvignon Blanc works splendidly with the feta and orzo salad as well, as it pairs nicely with goat's and sheep's milk cheeses.

Chicken Loaves with Marsala-Mushroom Sauce

CHRIS BENNETT

Who doesn't like the comfort of homemade meat loaf? And who says meat loaf has to be made with beef, pork, or lamb? I serve this chicken loaf accompanied by soft polenta and crisp asparagus. The next day, any leftovers are sliced for sandwiches on rustic bread and dressed with a tangy sweet hot mustard and some arugula or baby lettuces.

SERVES 4

CHICKEN LOAVES

2 tablespoons extra virgin olive oil

½ cup finely chopped onion

2 pounds ground chicken

½ cup finely chopped celery

¼ cup minced Italian parsley leaves

1½ teaspoons minced garlic

2 large eggs

¼ cup milk

¼ cup grated Parmigiano-Reggiano cheese

½ cup fresh bread crumbs

MARSALA-MUSHROOM SAUCE

¼ cup extra virgin olive oil

6 cloves garlic, coarsely chopped

1 cup sliced white mushrooms

1 cup Marsala

1 cup low-sodium chicken broth

2 tablespoons unsalted butter

MAKE THE CHICKEN LOAVES: Heat the oil in a saucepan over medium-low heat. Add the onion and sauté until translucent, 3 to 5 minutes. Transfer to a mixing bowl and allow the onion to cool. Add the chicken, celery, parsley, garlic, eggs, milk, cheese, and bread crumbs, and mix well. Cover and refrigerate until chilled, about 1 hour.

Divide the chicken mixture into 4 equal portions and, with wet hands, shape into small oval loaves about 1 inch high.

MAKE THE MARSALA-MUSHROOM SAUCE: Heat the oil in a large deep skillet (at least 12 inches in diameter) over medium-low heat. Add the garlic and sauté until golden. Using a slotted spoon, remove and discard the garlic.

Add the chicken loaves to the pan and increase the heat to medium-high. Allow to cook until golden brown on the undersides, 2 to 3 minutes, then turn and brown the other sides. Add the mushrooms and Marsala and simmer until the liquid is reduced by half.

Add the broth. Cover, and cook until an instant-read thermometer inserted in the center of the loaves registers 170°F, about 20 minutes. Transfer the loaves to a warm platter, cover with aluminum foil, and keep warm.

Increase the heat under the pan to high, and boil the sauce until reduced by half, scraping up the bits on the bottom. Whisk in the butter and pour the sauce over the chicken loaves. Serve immediately.

Wine pairing There's a lot going on in this dish—the heavier, sweeter Marsala sauce versus the delicate, savory chicken loaves. Choose a medium-bodied and fruit-forward red wine that will respond to both, such as Barbera from Italy's Piedmont, a Pinot Noir from California, or a New World-style Spanish wine.

Chicken Quenelles with Morels

DAVID WALTUCK

David and Karen Waltuck have taken their passion for mushrooms and crafted a terrific menu at Chanterelle. Quenelles are traditionally made with fish, but David uses ground chicken. These dumplings, poached in chicken stock, are accompanied by a mushroom sauce further enhanced by the chef's own mushroom stock.

SERVES 4

MUSHROOM STOCK
MAKES ABOUT 4 CUPS

10 cups chicken stock or water

1 onion, unpeeled, cut into chunks

3 carrots, unpeeled, cut into chunks

2 heads garlic, halved crosswise

2 cups mixed dried mushrooms, pulverized in
    a food processor

1 cup chopped fresh white mushrooms (or
    mushroom stems and trimmings)

QUENELLES

¾ pound skinless, boneless chicken breasts,
    cut into ½-inch chunks

1½ teaspoons salt

1 large egg white

2 cups heavy cream

1 teaspoon Madeira

Pinch of ground nutmeg

Pinch of cayenne pepper

2 cups chicken broth

MORELS AND SAUCE

2 tablespoons butter

1 pound fresh morel mushrooms, halved,
    rinsed in cold water, and drained

1 cup mushroom stock

2 tablespoons Madeira

1 cup heavy cream

1 teaspoon minced fresh tarragon

1 teaspoon minced fresh parsley

1 teaspoon minced fresh chervil

1 teaspoon minced fresh chives

MAKE THE MUSHROOM STOCK: In a large stockpot, combine the chicken stock, onion, carrots, garlic, dried mushrooms, and fresh mushrooms. Bring to a boil over high heat, decrease the heat to low, and simmer for 1½ hours.

Pour the broth through a strainer lined with cheesecloth into a container. Refrigerate any stock not used immediately for up to 1 week or freeze for up to 3 months.

PREPARE THE QUENELLES: In a food processor, combine the chicken, salt, and egg white. Process until puréed. With the machine running, gradually add the cream until the mixture is combined and fluffy. Pass the mixture through a fine-meshed sieve, pressing it through with the back of a wooden spoon. Add the Madeira, nutmeg, and cayenne, and process again until just blended. Cover and refrigerate until well chilled, about 1 hour.

Bring the chicken broth to a simmer in a medium saucepan over medium-low heat. Using 2 oval serving spoons, form 8 dumplings by scooping up some of the chicken mixture in one spoon and inverting the second spoon lightly over the first to shape the quenelle. Drop the quenelles into the chicken broth without crowding them, and poach for 8 minutes, turning once halfway through. (If desired, the broth and cooked quenelles may be cooled, covered, and refrigerated for up to 24 hours. Return to medium-low heat and reheat before continuing.)

MAKE THE MORELS AND SAUCE: Melt the butter in a medium skillet over low heat. Add the morels and sauté just until they are softened, then remove the pan from the heat. Drain off and reserve the pan liquid, then return the pan with the mushrooms to medium heat. Sauté for 1 to 2 minutes to dry out the mushrooms, then transfer the mushrooms to a plate. Pour the reserved liquid from the pan through a fine-meshed strainer lined with cheesecloth. Set aside.

In a wide shallow skillet, combine the reserved mushroom liquid, mushroom stock, and Madeira over medium-high heat and reduce to about half its volume. Add the morels, cream, and poached quenelles and cook until the sauce is slightly thickened, 7 to 8 minutes. Stir in the chopped tarragon, parsley, chervil, and chives.

To serve, place 2 quenelles on each of 4 rimmed plates or shallow soup plates. Top each with an equal portion of morels and sauce, and serve immediately.

Wine pairing An earthy Pinot Noir from the Willamette Valley in Oregon picks up the mushroom flavors and adds a bright cherry fruit for balance.

Roasted Quail
Stuffed with Figs and Prosciutto

BERTRAND BOUQUIN

Perfect as a first course, this tender quail melds lovingly with the fresh sweet figs and savory prosciutto. Protected by the prosciutto, the figs maintain their fresh flavor and do not become overcooked. When checking the quail for doneness, don't be fooled by the pink prosciutto; make sure that the juices run clear when pierced at the drumstick.

SERVES 4

4 to 5 tablespoons extra virgin olive oil

2 bunches (about 20) baby turnips, peeled,
   with ½ inch of stem attached

Salt and freshly ground black pepper

4 cups chicken stock, or as needed

4 fresh Black Mission figs, stems removed

4 very thin slices prosciutto

4 semi-boneless quail

2 pounds baby spinach leaves, washed and
   well dried

1 (14- to 16-ounce) jar piquillo (Spanish sweet)
   peppers, drained

Place a large sauté pan over medium-high heat, and add 1 tablespoon of the olive oil, the turnips, and salt and pepper to taste. Sauté until the turnips begin to soften but not brown, about 5 minutes. Add just enough chicken stock to barely cover the turnips. Simmer until the turnips are tender, about 8 minutes. Remove from the heat and keep warm.

Preheat the oven to 400°F. Wrap a fig in a slice of prosciutto and stuff it into a quail. Insert a toothpick through the drumsticks to secure the fig inside the quail. Season with salt and pepper. Repeat with the remaining figs, slices of prosciutto, and quail.

Place a large ovenproof sauté pan over high heat. When the pan is hot, add 1 tablespoon of the olive oil. Add the quail and sear on every side until well browned. Transfer to the oven and cook, basting every 2 minutes, until clear juices run when the quail are pierced at the leg joints, about 10 minutes.

Again, place a large sauté pan or other very wide pan over high heat. When the pan is hot, add 1 tablespoon of the olive oil. Add the spinach and cook quickly, tossing until it is just wilted, 1 to 2 minutes. Season with salt and pepper to taste. Drain well, and keep warm.

Place the piquillo peppers in a blender, and blend them with just enough olive oil (1 to 2 tablespoons) to obtain the consistency of a coulis (a thick sauce). Season with salt and pepper to taste.

To serve, divide the spinach among 4 plates and top with a quail. Arrange a serving of turnips around each quail and drizzle the piquillo pepper coulis around the turnips. Serve immediately.

Wine pairing Pick the star flavor in this elegant quail dish—the piquillo peppers—for the wine match. Try a Carmenère from Chile or a Cru Bourgeois from Bordeaux; either will singularly handle the peppers and support the interweaving tastes of mild quail, salty prosciutto, and vibrant fig.

Roasted Turkey Breast with Endive, Apples, and Walnuts

DANIEL BOULUD

If you're in the mood for turkey but not for the whole bird, Daniel Boulud's flavor-infused turkey breast couldn't be more satisfying. His presentation, even in the cooking stage, is lovely, with a strip of bay leaves surrounding the turkey and enclosed with tempting bacon strips. There's a yin-yang flavor going on with the endive and apples, bitter and sweet all wrapped up in a terrific, innovative entrée.

SERVES 6

1 (5- to 6-pound) whole turkey breast, bone
    removed and reserved

4 large bay leaves, broken lengthwise in half

8 slices bacon

Salt and crushed black peppercorns

3 tablespoons extra virgin olive oil

½ cup water

1 tablespoon sherry vinegar

¼ cup walnut oil

10 medium Belgian endive, trimmed,
    halved lengthwise, and cut crosswise
    into ½-inch-thick pieces

2 medium Fuji apples, peeled, cored, and
    julienned

1 bunch Italian parsley (leaves only)

½ cup toasted walnuts

Freshly ground black pepper

Preheat the oven to 425°F. Cut the turkey breast in half and place horizontally, skin side up, on a cutting board. Place 4 bay leaf halves crosswise along the center of one breast half. Secure each bay leaf by wrapping a slice of bacon around it; tie with kitchen string. (The bay leaves must be completely covered to keep them from burning.) Repeat with the second breast, then season both breasts with salt and crushed black pepper.

Put the olive oil in a medium roasting pan over high heat. When the oil is hot, add the turkey pieces to the pan, skin side down, and brown for about 5 minutes on one side. Turn the breasts over and cook until evenly browned, about 15 minutes more. Remove the breasts from the pan, pour off the fat, and add the breast bones. Arrange the breasts, skin side down, on top of the bones. Roast for 20 minutes. Turn the breasts over and roast for about 20 minutes more, or until an instant-read thermometer inserted into the center of a breast reaches 150°F. Transfer the breasts to a warm platter and keep warm.

Discard the bones and skim off the fat from the pan juices. Put the roasting pan on the stove, add the water, and bring to a boil. Reduce the liquid, stirring and scraping, until 2 tablespoons remain. Strain through a fine-meshed sieve into a medium bowl and whisk in the vinegar and walnut oil to make a vinaigrette.

Toss together the endive, apples, parsley, and walnuts in a large bowl and season to taste with salt and ground pepper. Add enough vinaigrette to lightly coat the salad.

To serve, carefully remove the kitchen string and bay leaves from the turkey. Arrange the salad on a large platter and top with the breasts for carving tableside. Drizzle the remaining vinaigrette over all.

Wine pairing Any number of wines can be successfully paired with turkey, so for this recipe focus on the accompaniments—apple and walnuts. For red, pour a Dolcetto d'Alba; white, a Chardonnay from Côte de Beaune or Sonoma County; or perhaps a rosé from Provence.

Sautéed Chicken with Cabernet Wine Vinegar Sauce

BERNARD DERVIEUX

If you have the luxury of using a cabernet vinegar, you'll appreciate its special taste. Several of my fellow Napa vintners produce terrific aged vinegars that provide deeper, richer flavors than you might get with a generic variety. Bernard's method of preparing the chicken—searing and quickly oven-roasting it almost at a broil—seals in the juices and cuts cooking time to a minimum.

SERVES 4

2 large whole chickens, cut into serving pieces, or chicken parts (such as 4 chicken breasts or 4 whole legs with thighs attached)

Salt and freshly ground black pepper

2 tablespoons butter

4 cloves garlic, unpeeled

2 tablespoons chopped shallots

3 tablespoons red wine

3 tablespoons Cabernet wine vinegar (Sources, see page 164)

1 cup chicken stock

2 tomatoes, cored and diced

Chopped fresh chives or Italian parsley, for garnish

Preheat the oven to 500°F. Sprinkle the chicken pieces on all sides with salt and pepper.

Place a large ovenproof skillet over medium heat and melt 1 tablespoon of the butter. Add the chicken parts, skin side down, and the garlic cloves. Raise the heat to medium-high, and sauté the chicken, turning as needed until browned on all sides.

Transfer the skillet to the oven and cook until the chicken is cooked through, about 15 minutes. (Alternatively, cover the skillet, decrease the heat to medium-low, and cook slowly on the stovetop until the chicken is tender.)

Transfer the chicken to a platter. Discard all but 1 tablespoon of the drippings from the skillet. Add the shallots and sauté until lightly browned. Add the wine and vinegar and cook until the liquid is reduced by half. Add the chicken stock and tomatoes. Season with salt and pepper. Stir in the remaining 1 tablespoon of butter.

Return the chicken to the sauce until thoroughly reheated, 1 to 2 minutes. Sprinkle with chives, and serve immediately.

Wine pairing Complement the Cabernet sauce with another Cabernet, but choose one from Sonoma County or Chile that has a medium body and soft tannins.

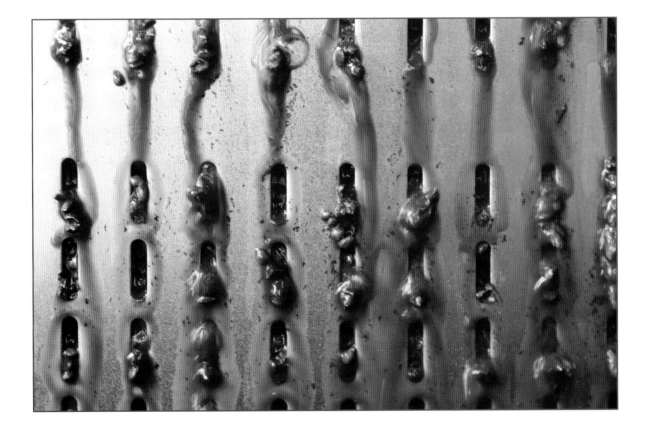

Side Dishes

Baked Wild Rice with Onion and Pecans

BARBARA BRYANT

This wild rice dish is a staple side in my repertoire. Assemble it early in the day or a day ahead, refrigerate, and bake just before serving. Serve as an accompaniment to Braised Short Ribs (page 70), Chicken Loaves with Marsala-Mushroom Sauce (page 98), or Peppered Beef Tenderloin (page 78).

SERVES 6 TO 8

5 tablespoons butter, plus additional for
    buttering pan
1 pound small white mushrooms, stemmed
1 medium yellow onion, chopped
1 cup chopped pecans
1 cup wild rice, rinsed
3 cups chicken broth
Salt and freshly ground black pepper

Preheat the oven to 350°F. Butter a shallow 2-quart covered casserole and set aside.

In a large sauté pan over low heat, melt 2 tablespoons of the butter. Add the mushrooms and sauté until they are browned and release their juices. Continue to cook until the juices are reduced and the pan is nearly dry. Transfer the mushrooms to a platter and return the unwashed pan to the stovetop over medium-low heat.

Add 2 tablespoons of the butter and the onions. Sauté until the onions are translucent, 2 to 3 minutes. Transfer the onion to the platter with the mushrooms, and again return the unwashed pan to the stovetop over medium heat.

Add the remaining 1 tablespoon of butter and the pecans. Sauté the pecans until fragrant and toasted, about 2 minutes. Stir in the rice, broth, mushrooms, and onion. Season with salt and pepper to taste.

Transfer the rice mixture to the casserole. Cover and bake until the rice is just tender, about 1 hour. Serve hot.

Wine pairing An Oregon Pinot Noir will hold up nicely to the nuttiness in both the pecans and the wild rice.

Broccoli Custard

RICHARD PERRY

Richard's broccoli custard is the ultimate comfort food. It also works well as a vegetarian main course with a salad of bitter greens that includes arugula, radicchio, and endive.

SERVES 6 AS A LUNCHEON COURSE

6 cups small broccoli florets

6 large eggs, beaten

8 cups heavy cream

1 tablespoon salt

1 teaspoon freshly ground black pepper

¾ cup diced green bell pepper

¾ cup diced red bell pepper

6 tablespoons minced onion

Bring a large pot of water to a boil, add the broccoli, and cook just until it turns bright green, 20 to 30 seconds. Drain immediately and plunge the broccoli into the ice water to chill and retain its bright green color. Drain well.

Preheat the oven to 350°F. In a large mixing bowl, stir together the eggs, cream, salt, and pepper. Mix in the green and red peppers, onion, and broccoli.

Pour the mixture into a shallow 6-quart baking dish. Bake until the custard is set and a knife inserted 2 inches from the edge comes out clean, 30 to 60 minutes depending on the depth and shape of the baking dish. Let cool for a few minutes, then slice, and serve hot.

Wine pairing A Grüner Veltliner from the Wachau or Kamptal regions of Austria will stand up gracefully to strong-flavored vegetables like broccoli. These wines include an array of flavors, including tropical fruits, grapefruit, and a peppery note, all bound with a good acidity.

Brown Butter and Chive Grits

LARRY FORGIONE AND JOSH GALLIANO

To my mind, there's no bad way to serve grits. Look for the stone-ground variety for a defined texture. Larry's recipe elevates this oft-maligned food from the ordinary to the sublime.

SERVES 4

2 cups skim milk

⅓ cup finely diced onion

2½ cups water

1 cup stone-ground grits, such as Anson Mills Antebellum Grits

½ cup (1 stick) butter

Salt and freshly ground black pepper

¼ cup finely sliced fresh chives

Wine pairing These buttery grits are a wonderful match with a Riesling or Pinot Blanc from Alsace.

In a large heavy pot, combine the milk, onion, and water. Place over medium-high heat and bring to a boil, then whisk in the grits. Decrease the heat to low and constantly whisk for the first few minutes to ensure that the grits do not stick to the bottom of the pot. Cook the grits until they are tender, 30 to 40 minutes depending on the brand and texture of grits.

While the grits are cooking, heat the butter in a skillet until golden brown but not burned. Immediately pour the butter into a heatproof bowl, and set aside.

When the grits are cooked, mix them in the browned butter and season with salt and pepper to taste. Stir in the sliced chives and serve immediately.

Roasted Brussels Sprouts with Pancetta

JAMES FIALA

While Jimmy's Brussels sprouts are our family's favorite Thanksgiving vegetable, my children beg for them year-round. We even eat them cold as a snack. This recipe is easy to prepare and is lovely served with roasted meats or poultry. They can also be tossed with pasta.

SERVES 6 TO 8

3 pounds Brussels sprouts

7 ounces pancetta, cut into small dice

3 tablespoons unsalted butter

Salt and freshly ground black pepper

1 to 2 tablespoons extra virgin olive oil

Preheat the oven to 400°F. Trim the root ends off the Brussels sprouts and remove any yellowed or dry outer leaves. Cut the sprouts into quarters.

Place a heavy ovenproof skillet over medium heat and cook the pancetta. When the pancetta is lightly browned, add the sprouts, butter, and salt to taste. Sauté until the sprouts are lightly browned, about 2 minutes.

Transfer the skillet to the oven and roast until the sprouts are brown on the outside and soft inside, 7 to 10 minutes. Transfer to a warm serving bowl, and season with salt and pepper to taste. Drizzle with the olive oil and serve.

Wine pairing Try a medium-bodied red from the region of Tuscany, Languedoc, or the southern Rhône, such as a Châteauneuf-du-Pape.

Carrot Farro

MICHAEL ANTHONY

Farro, a popular grain from the Tuscany region of Italy, is becoming better known on this side of the ocean as chefs like Michael Anthony introduce to it to their customers. Cooked like rice, farro has a chewy texture like wheat berries that goes well with the sweet, soft carrots here.

SERVES 10

2 tablespoons olive oil

4 cups diced onion

1 pound farro

Salt and freshly ground black pepper

2 pounds yellow and orange carrots, sliced

1 to 2 tablespoons extra virgin olive oil

Salt and freshly ground black pepper

3 cups Thumbelina or baby carrots, peeled, trimmed, and halved

1 cup frozen shelled edamame (soybeans)

1 cup carrot juice

½ cup freshly squeezed orange juice

1 cup toasted pine nuts

Salt and freshly ground black pepper

To make the farro, place a large saucepan over medium heat, and add the olive oil and onion. Sauté until softened but not browned. Add the farro and sauté until lightly browned. Add enough water just to cover. Decrease the heat to low and simmer, stirring occasionally, until the farro is tender, about 30 minutes; add more water as necessary to prevent scorching. Remove from the heat and season with salt and pepper to taste.

In a large saucepan, toss the sliced carrots in olive oil and sprinkle with salt and pepper. Cover and cook over low heat until very tender, about 10 minutes. Purée in a blender, and season with salt and pepper.

Place the halved carrots in a steamer and cook until crisp-tender. Remove and allow to cool. Steam the edamame just until bright green. Remove and allow to cool.

In a large bowl, combine the carrot juice, orange juice, carrot purée, and farro. Add more salt and pepper if necessary. Garnish with the baby carrots, pine nuts, and edamame. Serve at room temperature.

Wine pairing With these chewy grains and soft carrots, try a crisp, dry Verdicchio from the Marches region of Italy, just south of the Veneto region.

Foie Gras Risotto

CHRISTOPHER MANNING

This incredibly rich and creamy, yet delicate, starter is perfect for an intimate New Year's Eve dinner. Christopher Manning has a gift for surprising the palate, as he shows in this elegant dish.

SERVES 4

3 cups chicken stock

1 tablespoon unsalted butter

1 tablespoon finely diced shallot

1 tablespoon finely diced onion

¾ cup Arborio rice

1 cup Chandon Brut Classic or other
    sparkling wine

½ cup heavy cream

¼ pound (4 ounces) foie gras (Sources,
    see page 164)

Salt and freshly ground black pepper

¼ cup finely grated Pecorino Romano cheese

Wine pairing Pair this rich risotto with a sweet red Recioto della Valpolicella from Italy or a Pinot Noir from California's Russian River Valley.

Place the chicken stock in a small saucepan over low heat and bring to a simmer; keep warm. In a medium saucepan or Dutch oven, melt the butter and add the shallot and onion. Cover, stirring occasionally, and cook until the onion is tender but not browned. Add the rice and stir until evenly coated with the butter.

Add the sparkling wine, and stir constantly until the wine is almost gone. Stir in ½ cup of the chicken stock, letting the liquid absorb. Continue to stir in the stock, about ¼ cup at a time, letting the rice absorb the stock before adding the next amount. Cook the risotto until al dente; the rice should be slightly chewy.

Warm the cream in a small saucepan over low heat and using a blender, blend in the foie gras until smooth. Add the foie gras cream to the rice, stir well, and season with salt and pepper. Divide the risotto among 4 serving bowls, garnish with the cheese, and serve.

Herbed Ricotta

CELINA TIO

Homemade ricotta cheese is easy to make, and I'm grateful to Celina Tio for sharing her recipe. While this goes with Mushroom Stacks (page 56), the cheese also can be used in lasagna or as a filling for ravioli or stuffed shells.

MAKES ABOUT 4 OUNCES

4 cups whole milk

1 tablespoon white wine vinegar

½ teaspoon chopped fresh Italian parsley

½ teaspoon chopped fresh tarragon

½ teaspoon chopped fresh thyme

1 tablespoon unsalted butter, melted

⅛ teaspoon baking soda

Salt and freshly ground black pepper

Wine pairing The herbs and mild cheese are complemented with a German Spätlese Riesling.

Line a large-holed strainer with a double layer of cheesecloth, and set aside. Bring water in the bottom half of a double boiler to a boil. Clip a candy or deep-fry thermometer to the side of the top half of the double boiler, and heat the milk to 200°F. Remove from the heat and stir in the vinegar. The milk will coagulate quickly.

Pour the curd into the strainer, leaving it for only a minute or two; the cheese should be loose, but with no curds seeping from the edges. Transfer to a bowl.

Mix in the parsley, tarragon, thyme, butter, and baking soda. Season with salt and pepper to taste. Use immediately, or cover and refrigerate until needed.

Goat Cheese and Potato-Stuffed Artichoke Bottoms with Truffles

BILL CARDWELL

Serve this unique side dish with a grilled rib-eye steak. The filling—perfect on artichoke bottoms—can also be used as a filling for large mushroom caps, phyllo cups, or potato skins.

SERVES 6

2 large Yukon gold potatoes, scrubbed
    and unpeeled

6 cloves garlic, peeled

½ cup fresh goat cheese

¼ cup heavy cream

2 tablespoons minced fresh chives, plus more
    for garnish

1 teaspoon minced fresh tarragon

1 teaspoon truffle oil

Salt and freshly ground black pepper

6 fresh or canned artichoke bottoms

1 small black truffle or summer truffle, shaved
    into thin slices, for garnish (optional)

In a large saucepan or Dutch oven, combine the potatoes and garlic with just enough lightly salted water to cover the potatoes. Bring to a boil over high heat, then decrease the heat to medium and cook until the potatoes are just tender when pierced with a knife, about 20 minutes. Drain and allow to dry out slightly.

Preheat the oven to 350°F. In a medium bowl, coarsely mash the potatoes with the goat cheese, cream, chives, tarragon, and truffle oil. Season with salt and pepper.

Divide the potato mixture among the artichoke bottoms. Place in a baking pan and bake on the center rack of the oven for about 10 minutes. Remove from the oven, top with chives and, if desired, shavings of truffle. Serve immediately.

Wine pairing Enjoy a Cabernet Sauvignon from Chile with these potatoes; if you prefer white wines, pair with a white Côtes du Rhône.

Chanterelles and Fingerling Potatoes with Tarragon

JULIE RIDLON

Julie Ridlon, like many chefs featured in this book, supports local farmers. She has been instrumental in the Chef's Collaborative and other groups that connect chefs with farmers and local communities. Julie started the Clayton Farmer's Market in St. Louis, just down the street from me. If I get there early enough on a Saturday morning, I can find the fingerlings for this dish.

SERVES 6 TO 8

¼ cup light olive oil

2 pounds fingerling potatoes, cut into ½-inch slices (or Yukon gold potatoes)

4 tablespoons (½ stick) unsalted butter

½ pound chanterelle mushrooms, cleaned and halved, or quartered if large

2 tablespoons chopped fresh tarragon

Salt and freshly ground black pepper

Heat the olive oil in a large sauté pan or skillet over medium-high heat. Add the potatoes and sauté until softened and lightly browned, 10 to 15 minutes, stirring occasionally.

Decrease the heat to medium and add the butter and chanterelles. Sauté for 10 minutes, adjusting the heat as necessary to prevent burning. The mushrooms will give up their juices, then absorb them again and begin to brown. In the last minutes of cooking, add the tarragon, and season with salt and pepper to taste. Serve hot.

Wine pairing Try a Chardonnay from Chassagne-Montrachet in Burgundy to show off the flavors of the subtle chanterelles and the nutty, firm texture of the fingerlings.

Pan-Roasted Cipollini Onions with Bacon and Fresh Daikon Radish

ALEXANDRA GUARNASCHELLI

When I asked Alexandra for a contribution, she sent this recipe, along with a note: "I combined these ingredients because they accompany a piece of steak or hearty fish nicely. The onions are slightly sweet and the bacon salty. The radish, warmed slightly with the other elements, gives a delicate, peppery bite. I also feel that, once cooked and blended, these ingredients illuminate the different qualities of a fine Cabernet." I couldn't agree more.

SERVES 4

12 slices bacon (preferably with a slightly
    smoky flavor)

32 cipollini onions, peeled and trimmed

Sea salt and freshly ground pepper

1 cup red wine

2 cups water

2 teaspoons vegetable oil

6 ounces daikon radish, peeled and cut into
    1-inch "Scrabble chip" squares

1 tablespoon balsamic vinegar

Place the bacon slices flat on a cutting board. Cut them into 1-inch squares similar in size to the pieces of radish. Heat a large sauté pan over medium-low heat and cook the bacon until light brown. Using a slotted spoon or spatula, transfer the bacon to paper towels to drain. Return the unwashed pan, with the bacon fat, to medium-low heat.

Place the onions in a single layer in the pan. Season with salt and pepper to taste. Cook until lightly browned on the underside. Using a spatula, turn the onions over and add the wine. Cook until all of the wine has evaporated. Add the water. Raise the heat slightly and cook the onions until they are tender when pierced in the center with the tip of a small knife. (Note: Sometimes onions take a long time to cook. If all of the water reduces and the onions are still firm, add a little more liquid until they are fully cooked.)

In a small sauté pan, heat the oil over medium heat. Add the daikon radish and cook for 1 minute, tossing with a wooden spoon so the radish softens slightly. Season with salt and pepper.

When the onions are tender, drain off any excess liquid in the pan. Add the balsamic vinegar and cook for 1 minute. Add the radishes and stir to blend. Add the bacon pieces and toss to mix.

Spoon the mixture into a large dish and serve it family style. Alternatively, divide the mixture onto 4 plates.

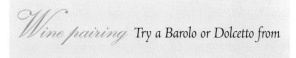

Wine pairing Try a Barolo or Dolcetto from Italy's Piedmont region.

Roasted Garlic and Almond Flan
with Asparagus and Wild Mushrooms

BRYAN CARR

Bryan Carr refers to this savory flan as "deep and voluptuous." He serves it with lamb and wild mushrooms, but it's good enough to stand on its own for dinner or brunch when accompanied by a green salad tossed with a shallot vinaigrette.

SERVES 6

¼ cup olive oil

6 large cloves garlic

1 cup blanched almonds

3 cups heavy cream

8 large egg yolks

Salt and ground white pepper

Nonstick cooking spray

6 tablespoons butter

18 ounces mixed mushrooms, (such as white, shiitake, or chanterelle)

Juice of 1 lemon

¼ cup chopped fresh Italian parsley

¼ cup chopped fresh chives

Salt and freshly ground black pepper

36 tender stalks asparagus, woody ends trimmed

¼ cup melted unsalted butter

Salt

MAKE THE FLAN: Preheat the oven to 250°F. Place a small heavy saucepan over very low heat. Add the olive oil and garlic, and cook, stirring occasionally, until the garlic is very soft but not browned, about 30 minutes. Meanwhile, place a medium skillet over medium-low heat and add the almonds. Stir with a wooden spoon until the almonds are fragrant and lightly browned. Transfer to a plate and set aside.

When the garlic is tender, drain the pan of all the oil, add the cream and toasted almonds. Place over medium heat and bring to a simmer, then remove the mixture from the heat and allow to rest for 10 minutes. Purée in a blender, and pour through a fine-meshed strainer into a large mixing bowl. Add the egg yolks and stir until blended. Season to taste with salt and white pepper.

Fill a kettle with water and bring to a boil. Spray 6 ramekins with nonstick cooking spray. Divide the flan mixture among the ramekins and place in a large baking pan, adding enough boiling water to come halfway up the sides. Transfer to the oven and bake until set, about 1 hour. Remove the pan from the oven and let the flans rest in the hot water.

PREPARE THE MUSHROOMS: Place a large heavy skillet over high heat until quite hot. Add the butter and, when it begins to brown, add the mushrooms. Sauté until they give up their juices, absorb them again, and become lightly browned. Add the lemon juice, parsley, and chives. Toss and cook for 1 minute more. Season with salt and black pepper; set aside, keeping warm.

PREPARE THE ASPARAGUS: Bring a large pot of water to a boil. Add the asparagus and boil just until bright green and tender-crisp, 2 to 3 minutes. (Be careful not to overcook; cooking time will vary depending on the thickness of the asparagus.) Drain the asparagus, brush with the melted butter, and season with salt to taste.

To serve, invert the ramekins in the center of each of 6 plates. Spoon the hot mushrooms around the flans and arrange the asparagus over the mushrooms.

Wine pairing With the delicate flavors of flan, asparagus, and mushrooms, introduce fresh Fino Sherry, served chilled.

Desserts

Almond Biscotti

BARBARA BRYANT

When I need a quick dessert or something sweet for an impromptu tea, fresh-cut fruit and these almond biscotti are my standards—so I like to always keep a batch in the freezer. Add the zest of 1 lemon and 2 teaspoons lemon juice for a tart version.

MAKES 4 DOZEN COOKIES

3 cups all-purpose flour

3 teaspoons baking powder

3 large eggs

1 teaspoon vanilla extract

1 cup sugar

½ cup (1 stick) butter, at room temperature

¼ teaspoon salt

1 tablespoon almond paste

1 cup whole almonds, coarsely chopped

Sift the flour and baking powder together in a bowl and set aside. Using an electric mixer or by hand, mix together the eggs and vanilla. Add the sugar, butter, salt, almond paste, and almonds; mix well.

Add the flour mixture to the egg mixture, and mix well to make a dough. Cover with plastic wrap and refrigerate until firm, up to 48 hours.

Preheat the oven to 350°F. Butter a baking sheet or line with parchment paper. Shape the dough into 3 rectangular loaves, each about 2½ inches wide, 1 inch high, and 9 inches long. Place the loaves about 3 inches apart on the baking sheet.

Bake the loaves for 5 to 6 minutes, then check to see if they need reshaping. If necessary, reshape the loaves with a spatula. Bake until very lightly browned on top, another 10 minutes. Let cool. (At this stage, the loaves may be wrapped airtight and frozen for up to 3 months.)

Butter another baking sheet or line with parchment paper. Cut the loaves into diagonal slices with a serrated knife and place, cut side down, 1 inch apart on the baking sheets. Bake until golden brown, 15 to 20 minutes. Cool completely and store in an airtight container.

Wine pairing Biscotti were created for dipping. There is no better way to enjoy these biscotti than to first baptize them in a glass of luxurious Vin Santo, considered by many to be the nectar of the gods.

Berries and Semolina Pudding

DAN BARBER

Dan Barber calls for strawberries, but I'm sure he would heartily endorse fresh blueberries, raspberries, currants, or a combination of any of them in this surprisingly light, cakelike pudding.

SERVES 8

4 tablespoons (½ stick), plus additional for
  buttering pan
1 cup semolina flour, plus additional for dusting
  pan
4 cups whole milk
Finely grated zest of ½ orange
Finely grated zest of ½ lemon
1 vanilla bean, split and pulp removed (pod
  discarded or reserved for another use)
5 large eggs, separated
¾ cup sugar
4 cups stemmed and quartered fresh
  strawberries

Wine pairing Moscato d'Asti is a light and refreshing sparkling wine that carries hints of citrus and strawberries. The slight carbonation balances the pudding and the trace of strawberry celebrates the berries.

Preheat the oven to 325°F. Butter a 9 by 13-inch baking pan and dust with semolina.

In a medium saucepan over low heat, combine the milk, orange zest, lemon zest, and vanilla bean pulp, and bring to a boil. Gradually whisk in the semolina until the mixture thickens. Whisk in the egg yolks and the butter. When the butter has melted and is completely incorporated, remove the pan from the heat. Transfer the batter to a large mixing bowl and set aside.

In the bowl of an electric mixer, combine the sugar and the egg whites. Whisk until soft peaks form. Using a rubber spatula, gently fold the egg whites into the semolina batter until fully incorporated and no streaks remain.

Pour the batter into the prepared pan. Bake until firm and lightly browned, about 30 minutes.

Transfer the pan to a wire rack to cool. Cut pudding into 8 portions and serve warm or at room temperature, topped with the strawberries.

Blueberry Tart with Crème Fraîche

BARBARA BRYANT

As a mother of three, I have happily devoted much time in the kitchen to preparing comfort food for family meals and gatherings with friends. This tart is a family favorite.

SERVES 8

CRUST

½ cup (1 stick) unsalted butter, at room temperature

1 cup all-purpose flour

2 tablespoons granulated sugar

Pinch of salt

1 tablespoon white vinegar

½ cup granulated sugar

2 tablespoons all-purpose flour

½ teaspoon freshly squeezed lemon juice

¼ teaspoon ground cinnamon

2 cups fresh blueberries

1 cup fresh blueberries

Confectioners' sugar, for dusting

Zest of 1 lemon

1 cup crème fraîche

Preheat the oven to 400°F. Butter a 9-inch springform pan and set aside. In a medium bowl, whisk together the flour, sugar, and salt. Add the butter and vinegar, working it in with your fingers until pea-size lumps form. Press the mixture onto the bottom of the pan and up the sides.

In a medium bowl, whisk together the sugar, flour, lemon juice, and cinnamon. Stir in 2 cups of the blueberries. Pour the filling into the crust. Bake until firm and lightly golden on top, about 1 hour. Transfer to a wire rack to cool slightly.

Sprinkle the remaining 1 cup of blueberries over the cake while it is still warm. Remove the rim of the springform pan and transfer the cake to a serving platter. Dust with confectioners' sugar and sprinkle with lemon zest. Serve warm with a dollop of crème fraîche.

Wine pairing A light, airy Asti Spumante is a proper complement to this tart's berries and custard.

Campfire Pie

CINDY PAWLCYN

Remember s'mores from the campfire days of your youth? Hot, roasted, almost burned marshmallows placed between two graham crackers with a few squares of a Hershey's chocolate bar? Cindy Pawlcyn has a knack for updating American favorites, like her pie version of s'mores, but made with Oreos, another classic.

MAKES TWO 9-INCH PIES
(8 SERVINGS FOR EACH PIE)

CRUSTS

1 (18-ounce) package Oreo cookies

12 tablespoons (1½ sticks) unsalted butter, melted

CHOCOLATE SAUCE

½ pound unsweetened chocolate (chopped or chips)

¼ pound semisweet chocolate (chopped or chips)

½ cup light corn syrup

½ cup (1 stick) unsalted butter, at room temperature

1¼ cups heavy cream

ALMOND DING

4 tablespoons (½ stick) unsalted butter

1 cup sugar

½ teaspoon salt

2 cups whole unsalted almonds

MARSHMALLOW FILLING

¾ cup water

¼ cup corn syrup

2¼ cups sugar

8 packages unflavored powdered gelatin, soaked in 1 cup cold water

1¼ cups egg whites (about 12)

⅜ teaspoon cream of tartar

1 tablespoon vanilla extract

4 cups coarsely crumbled Oreo cookies (about ½-inch pieces)

PREPARE THE CRUSTS: Using a food processor, pulverize the cookies into fine crumbs. Add the butter and pulse until blended. Press the mixture into two 9-inch pie pans and chill.

MAKE THE CHOCOLATE SAUCE: Bring water to a simmer in the bottom of a double boiler. In the top portion, melt together the unsweetened chocolate and semisweet chocolate. Stir in the corn syrup and butter and mix well, then stir in the cream. Set aside.

MAKE THE ALMOND DING: Grease a baking sheet or line with parchment paper, and set aside. In a large sauté pan, combine the butter, sugar, salt, and almonds. Cook over medium heat, stirring frequently, until the almonds are toasted and the caramel is a light brown. Pour onto the pan and allow to cool and harden. Using a metal spatula, loosen the cooled ding and break into small pieces.

Remove the crusts from the refrigerator and spread 6 tablespoons of the chocolate sauce on the bottom and sides of each crust.

MAKE THE MARSHMALLOW FILLING: In a large saucepan, combine the water, corn syrup, and sugar. Bring to a boil and cook to the soft-ball stage (235 to 240°F degrees on a candy thermometer). Meanwhile, place the gelatin in a 200°F oven (or a microwave at a low setting) to warm and soften it. Using an electric mixer, whisk the egg whites and cream of tartar to soft peaks. Increase the speed to high and slowly pour in the hot sugar syrup. Start with a very thin stream and increase as the whites heat up. Add the warmed gelatin and the vanilla and whisk until fairly stiff. Immediately start to fill the pies, as the mixture will set quickly.

Fill each pie with 2 cups marshmallow and top with about 1 cup cookie pieces, ¼ cup almond ding chips, and 4 tablespoons chocolate sauce. Repeat this layering. Finish with the remaining marshmallow and spread it around to cover the top. Chill. Warm the pies before serving and use a kitchen torch to brown the edges of the pie, or place under a broiler for about 10 seconds, or until very lightly browned.

Wine pairing There is nothing like countering the sweet memories of a youthful dessert with a grown-up glass of ruby-style port or late-harvest Black Muscat from California.

Chestnut Soufflé with Nutmeg Sauce

JEAN-GEORGES VONGERICHTEN

As chef-owner of Vong, JoJo, Jean Georges, Spice Market, and other restaurants around the world, Jean-Georges needs no introduction. These individual hot soufflés manage to be airy, creamy, sweet, and savory all at the same time. It's a show-offy dessert guaranteed to impress your guests.

SERVES 12

NUTMEG SAUCE

2 cups crème fraîche

5 tablespoons heavy cream

2 tablespoons Armagnac

1½ teaspoons vanilla extract

1½ teaspoons ground nutmeg

SOUFFLÉS

1⅛ cups milk

1 cup chestnut purée (Sources, see page 164)

¼ cup hazelnut flour (Sources, see page 164)

⅓ cup cornstarch

1 cup egg whites (about 8 large; do not use processed whites)

½ cup granulated sugar, plus additional for dusting ramekins

Butter for ramekins

12 candied chestnuts (marrons glacés) (Sources, see page 164)

Cocoa powder or confectioners' sugar, for dusting

MAKE THE NUTMEG SAUCE: In a small bowl, mix together the crème fraîche and heavy cream. Add the Armagnac, vanilla, and nutmeg. Mix well and refrigerate until serving.

MAKE THE SOUFFLÉS: Preheat the oven to 375°F. In a medium saucepan over medium heat, bring the milk to a simmer and whisk in the chestnut purée until very smooth. Remove from the heat and whisk in the hazelnut flour and cornstarch. Return to the stovetop and cook over low heat, stirring until thickened enough to mound when the whisk is lifted. Transfer to a bowl, cover with plastic wrap, and set aside at room temperature.

Using an electric mixer, whisk the egg whites with the sugar on low speed until they form soft peaks. Increase the speed to high and whisk for 2 minutes.

Add about 1 cup of egg white mixture to the chestnut base, gently whisking it to loosen the mixture. Using a flexible spatula, gently fold in the remaining whites, making sure to scrape the bottom of the bowl. Fold until smooth.

Butter twelve 4-ounce ramekins. Coat the interior of each ramekin with sugar. Place the chestnut mixture into a large pastry bag with a large plain tip. Pipe the mixture into the ramekins, filling them only halfway. Break 1 whole candied chestnut into pieces and place in the center of the batter. Pipe the remaining batter into the ramekins to fill them.

Place the ramekins on a baking sheet and bake until golden on top, 5 to 7 minutes. Dust with cocoa powder and serve immediately, passing the nutmeg sauce separately for spooning on top.

Wine pairing Choose a wine that responds to the heavenly nutmeg and ethereal qualities of this soufflé—a Vendange Tardive (late-harvest) Riesling or Muscat from Alsace.

Chocolate Decadence

NARSAI DAVID

Narsai David has become something of a legend for this recipe, and no wonder: it's just as he's named it—decadent, and outrageously delicious. Long before molten chocolate cake became the rage, Narsai invented Chocolate Decadence. Chocolate and red wine are a marriage made in heaven.

SERVES 12

10 tablespoons unsalted butter, plus additional
    for buttering pan
1 tablespoon all-purpose flour, plus additional for
    flouring pan
1 pound semisweet chocolate
1 tablespoon sugar
4 large eggs

3 cups fresh raspberries or 1 (¾-pound) package
    defrosted frozen raspberries
Sugar

1½ cups heavy cream
1 teaspoon vanilla extract
1 tablespoon sugar
Chocolate shavings, for garnish

MAKE THE CAKE: Preheat the oven to 450°F. Butter and flour an 8-inch springform pan, and line the bottom with parchment paper. Bring water to a simmer in the bottom of a double boiler. In the top portion or in a heatproof bowl set over the water, combine the chocolate and butter and stir just until melted. Remove from the heat and set aside.

In the double boiler or a heatproof bowl set over simmering water, whisk together the sugar and eggs just until the mixture is lukewarm; do not overcook. Remove from the heat and use an electric mixer to beat the mixture until it is quadrupled in volume.

Fold the flour into the sugar-egg mixture. Stir one-quarter of the egg mixture into the melted chocolate, then fold all of the chocolate back into the egg mixture. Pour into the prepared pan and bake for exactly 15 minutes; the cake will still be liquid in the center. Allow the cake to cool completely on a wire rack. Cover and freeze until solid, preferably overnight, before removing the cake from the pan.

PREPARE THE RASPBERRY SAUCE:
Purée the raspberries in a blender. Press through a fine-meshed sieve to remove the seeds. Add sugar to taste.

Using an electric mixer, whisk the cream, vanilla, and sugar until stiff peaks form.

TO SERVE: Unmold the cake by carefully dipping the bottom of the pan in hot water. (If there is any danger of water leaking into the pan, cover the bottom of the pan with plastic wrap before dipping it.) Transfer to a cake platter and cover the cake with the whipped cream. Decorate the top with shaved chocolate. Refrigerate for up to 1 hour before serving; the cake should be partially but not completely defrosted. Serve each slice in a pool of sweetened raspberry purée.

Wine pairing A rich and decadent Zinfandel Port has the weight and flamboyance of abundant ripe berry flavors to take on this level of chocolate.

Chocolate Mousse

DANIEL BOULUD

Everyone needs a great chocolate mousse recipe, and this one from Daniel Boulud is simple, yet classic. Use a top-quality chocolate; it will make a difference.

SERVES 6 TO 8

2¼ cups heavy cream

½ pound bittersweet chocolate, finely chopped

⅔ cup plus ½ cup sugar

¼ cup water

6 large eggs, separated

3 large eggs

Chocolate shavings, for serving

Whipped cream, for serving

Whip the cream in the bowl of an electric mixer fitted with the whisk attachment until it barely holds soft peaks; do not overwhip. Set aside.

Fill a saucepan halfway full with water and bring to a simmer. Put the bittersweet chocolate in a large bowl set over the pan of simmering water, making certain that the bottom of the bowl does not touch the water. Stir occasionally with a rubber spatula until the chocolate has melted and is hot. Remove from the heat and set aside.

Clip a candy thermometer to the side of a small, heavy saucepan. Combine ⅔ cup of the sugar and ¼ cup water in the saucepan. Place over medium-low heat and bring to a boil without stirring. Cover and boil until the sugar has completely dissolved. Uncover and let the mixture boil until it reaches the soft-ball stage, 240°F on the thermometer.

Meanwhile, in the bowl of an electric mixer fitted with the whisk attachment, beat the 6 egg yolks and 3 whole eggs until thick and pale. Pour the sugar syrup in a fine stream into the eggs, beating at high speed until the mixture is cool, 8 to 10 minutes. Transfer the egg mixture to another bowl. Wash the whisk and mixer bowl thoroughly and dry well.

Bring water to a bare simmer in a saucepan. Put the 6 egg whites into the clean, dry mixer bowl. While whisking, slowly add the remaining ½ cup sugar. Place the bowl over the barely simmering water, making certain that the bottom of the bowl does not touch the water, and stir until the mixture is hot to the touch. Attach the bowl to the mixer and whip with the whisk attachment, until the meringue holds tall, stiff, glossy peaks.

Fold one-third of the yolk mixture into the egg white mixture (meringue). Working very quickly, fold the reserved whipped cream into the hot melted chocolate (if the chocolate is not hot, rewarm over simmering water or in the microwave). Fold in the yolk mixture and then the meringue until just blended. Spoon the mousse into a large serving bowl and refrigerate until chilled, about 2 hours.

Serve family style, with chocolate shavings and whipped cream alongside in separate bowls.

Wine pairing Choose a bold, fruity, full-flavored red that can hold its own with this rich, decadent chocolate mousse. Perfect pairings include a late-bottled vintage Port or a Banyuls from Roussillon, France.

Cinnamon Panna Cotta with Apple Gelée, Goat's Milk Caramel, and Huckleberries

KEVIN NASHAN

Kevin Nashan's dessert makes a beautiful appearance. The gelatin mixed with the apple juice creates a sparkling, clear golden layer atop the panna cotta.

SERVES 8

PANNA COTTA

¼ vanilla bean, split lengthwise

8 cups heavy cream

1 cup brown sugar

2 cinnamon sticks

APPLE GELÉE

2½ cups clear (filtered) apple juice

3 (¼-ounce) packages unflavored powdered
    gelatin

GOAT'S MILK CARAMEL

4 cups goat's milk (available at specialty food
    stores or farmers' markets)

1 cup granulated sugar

2 sprigs thyme

1 star anise

¼ teaspoon baking soda

1 cup fresh huckleberries (Sources, see page 164)
    or blueberries

MAKE THE PANNA COTTA: Using the tip of a small paring knife, scrape the vanilla pulp into a large saucepan. Add the cream, brown sugar, and cinnamon sticks to the pan. Place over low heat and slowly bring to a simmer. Remove the pan from the heat and allow the ingredients to infuse for 20 minutes. Remove the cinnamon sticks and let the cream cool.

In a small saucepan, combine the gelatin with 1 cup of the cream. Place over low heat and stir until the gelatin is dissolved, 3 to 6 minutes. Add the mixture to the remaining cream and whisk to incorporate. Pour the mixture into a 2-quart serving dish to a depth of about 2 inches; there should be enough room left above the panna cotta for a thin layer of apple gelée. Chill for at least 4 hours in the refrigerator.

MAKE THE APPLE GELÉE: Once the panna cotta is firmly set, place 1 cup of the apple juice in a small saucepan over low heat. When the juice is very warm, remove from the heat and add the gelatin. Whisk until the gelatin is dissolved, and allow to cool completely. Gently pour the apple gelatin over the chilled panna cotta, and refrigerate again until the apple gelée has set, at least 2 hours.

COOK THE GOAT'S MILK CARAMEL: In a 2-quart saucepan, combine the goat's milk, sugar, thyme, and star anise. Place over medium-low heat and bring slowly to a boil. Whisking constantly, carefully add the baking soda; it will cause the milk to bubble quickly. Continue to cook, stirring frequently, until the caramel is smooth and golden brown, 30 to 45 minutes. Pour through a fine-meshed strainer, and keep warm.

Combine the huckleberries with the caramel in a decorative bowl or on a serving plate. Serve alongside the serving dish of panna cotta.

Wine pairing The apple and spice that define this extraordinary panna cotta call for a late-harvest, botrytised wine from Coteaux du Layon or a Bual Madeira.

Ginger-Molasses Spice Cake with Mascarpone and Clear Lady Apple Chips

CHARLIE TROTTER

Charlie Trotter is known for taking an old favorite—here spice cake—and putting a completely new spin on it. As he wrote to us: "This fragrant spice cake is perfect as a light ending to a substantial meal or as an early course in a dessert progression. The cake can even be served as a part of a breakfast menu because it is not very sweet. This is a great make-ahead preparation; the cake does not suffer in any way from being baked the day before." If Lady apples are not available, substitute any small cooking apple.

SERVES 9

APPLE CHIPS

1 cup granulated sugar

¼ cup freshly squeezed lemon juice

2 cups water

18 paper-thin slices Lady apples or other small apples (seeds removed, but not peeled or cored)

CAKE

Vegetable oil or nonstick vegetable spray, for greasing pan

2 cups all-purpose flour, plus additional for flouring pan

¼ cup freshly squeezed orange juice

¼ cup finely chopped fresh ginger

About ½ cup milk, as needed

2 tablespoons brandy

1½ teaspoons rice wine vinegar

½ cup (1 stick) unsalted butter

⅓ cup granulated sugar

2 large eggs

¾ cup light molasses

1½ teaspoons baking soda

¼ teaspoon salt

1 teaspoon ground cinnamon

⅛ teaspoon ground cloves

APPLES AND APPLE-GINGER SAUCE

2 cups granulated sugar

½ cup water

3 Lady apples, peeled, halved, cored, and cut into ⅛-inch slices

¼ cup finely chopped peeled fresh ginger

MASCARPONE CREAM

1 cup mascarpone cheese

½ cup heavy cream

2 tablespoons granulated sugar

Confectioners' sugar, for dusting

MAKE THE APPLE CHIPS: Preheat the oven to 225°F. Line a baking sheet with a nonstick liner or parchment paper. In a medium saucepan, combine the sugar, lemon juice, and water. Place over medium-low heat, bring to a simmer, and add the apple slices. Simmer until the slices are translucent, about 10 minutes. Remove the apple slices from the liquid and lay them flat on the baking sheet. Bake until the apples are thoroughly dry, 1 to 1½ hours. Carefully transfer the chips to a cooling rack. When completely cool, store in an airtight container at room temperature until ready to use.

MAKE THE CAKE: Preheat the oven to 350°F. Grease and flour a 9-inch square baking pan, then line with parchment paper. In a small saucepan, combine the orange juice and ginger. Place over low heat until the juice is warm, about 3 minutes. Remove from the heat, cover, and allow to steep for 30 minutes. Strain through a fine-meshed sieve and discard the ginger. Add enough milk to the orange juice to total ¾ cup of liquid, then add the brandy and vinegar.

Using an electric mixer, cream the butter and sugar until light and fluffy. Add the eggs and continue beating until they are fully incorporated. Add the molasses and beat until well mixed. Sift together the flour, baking soda, salt, cinnamon, and cloves. Alternately add the dry ingredients and the orange juice mixture to the batter, mixing well after each addition.

Pour the batter into the pan and bake until a toothpick inserted in the center of the cake comes out clean, 25 to 30 minutes. Transfer the cake to a wire rack to cool.

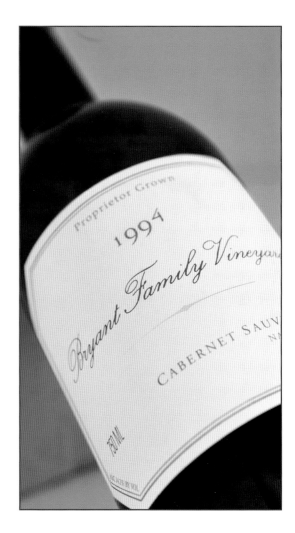

PREPARE THE APPLES AND APPLE-GINGER SAUCE: Cook the sugar and water in a medium heavy sauté pan over medium heat until golden brown and caramelized, about 10 minutes. Add the apple slices and simmer gently for 3 minutes. Using a wire skimmer or tongs, remove the apples, allowing any excess sauce to drip back into the pan; transfer to a bowl and set aside. Add the ginger to the pan. Boil until reduced by half, about 10 minutes. Strain through a fine-meshed sieve and discard the ginger; set aside.

MIX THE MASCARPONE CREAM: Using an electric mixer, whisk the mascarpone, cream, and sugar in a bowl until stiff peaks form. Cover and refrigerate until needed.

To serve, cut the cake into 2½-inch squares and use a round cutter to cut a 1-inch hole in the center of each piece. Lightly dust each dessert plate with confectioners' sugar and set a piece of cake in the center. Fill the hole in the cake with the mascarpone mixture and top with some of the warm apples. Spoon some of the mascarpone on top of the apples and stand 2 apple chips in the mascarpone. Drizzle the apple-ginger sauce around the plate.

Wine pairing This Old World dessert should be rewarded with no less than an aged tawny port, which has enough spice to enhance the cake's strong flavors. Australia has some very fine fortified Muscat wines from the Rutherglen region also worthy of Charlie's cake.

Chocolate Shortbread

BARBARA BRYANT

These shortbread cookies are a staple at our family's Christmas gatherings, but I make them all year, cutting them into hearts for Valentine's Day, stars at Christmas, and circles and squares for any all-occasion mixed cookie platter. I prefer Droste cocoa powder here; it's less acidic and imparts a soft reddish-brown color to the dough.

MAKES 6 DOZEN COOKIES

2 cups flour, sifted, plus additional flour
    for dusting
½ cup Dutch-processed cocoa, sifted
¼ teaspoon salt
1 cup (2 sticks) unsalted butter,
    at room temperature
1 teaspoon vanilla extract
1 cup confectioners' sugar

Preheat the oven to 300°F. Line baking sheets with nonstick silicone baking mats or parchment paper.

Sift together the flour, cocoa, and salt onto a piece of wax paper and set aside.

Cream the butter in an electric mixer at medium speed. Add the vanilla and confectioners' sugar and beat until well mixed. On low speed, add the flour mixture, beating just until the mixture holds together.

Lightly dust a clean countertop surface or marble pastry board with flour and knead the dough until perfectly smooth. Shape the dough into a ball and flatten it with the palm of your hand. Using a rolling pin, roll the dough to a ½-inch thickness.

Using a cookie cutter, cut the dough into desired shape(s) and place on the baking sheets.

Bake until the cookies look dry and are slightly firm to the touch, 20 to 25 minutes. Transfer the cookies to wire racks and allow to cool completely. Store in an airtight container. (The cookies can be frozen for up to 1 month.)

Wine pairing Bonny Doon produces a wonderful Framboise—a fortified wine made from raspberries—that is not too cloying and would be fantastic to sip while nibbling these cookies.

Crème Brûlée

SIRIO MACCIONI

No crème brûlée can top the classic version served at Le Cirque. It is the perfect finale to an elegant dinner party. Add fresh, seasonal berries to each plate for some additional color.

SERVES 9

1 cup packed brown sugar

1 vanilla bean

4 cups heavy cream

¾ cup granulated sugar

7 large egg yolks

Spread the brown sugar on a large plate or baking sheet and let dry, uncovered, for about 3 hours. When it is sufficiently dried, it will feel dry and sandy. Set aside.

Preheat the oven to 300°F. Split the vanilla bean in half lengthwise and scrape the pulp into a small saucepan. Add the vanilla pod, cream, and granulated sugar to the pan. Place over medium heat and stir until the mixture is heated and bubbles begin to form around the edge; do not allow it to boil. Remove from the heat.

In a large mixing bowl, whisk the egg yolks until blended. Continue to whisk while slowly pouring the hot cream mixture into the egg yolks. Whisk until the mixture is smooth and consistent in color. Pour the mixture through a fine-meshed sieve into a large measuring cup or bowl with a spout to remove the vanilla bean pieces and any bits of cooked egg.

Place nine 5-ounce ramekins on a baking sheet with 1-inch-high sides. Divide the custard among the ramekins; they should be filled to the brim, as the custard will lose volume as it bakes. Put the baking sheet in the oven and add enough hot tap water to the baking sheet to reach halfway up the sides of the ramekins. Bake until set, about 40 minutes. The baking time will vary depending on the depth of the ramekins; when baked correctly, the custard should tremble slightly when gently shaken.

Remove the ramekins from the water bath and place on a wire rack to cool for 30 minutes. Allow the water bath to cool before removing it from the oven. Cover the custards and refrigerate until well chilled, about 2 hours or up to 2 days. The custards will continue to firm up when chilled.

Just before serving, preheat the broiler. Press the dried brown sugar through a sieve to remove any lumps. Immediately before serving, spread a thin layer of the brown sugar (about 2 tablespoons) over the tops of the custards until the custard is no longer visible. Place the ramekins on a baking sheet about 4 inches under the broiler and broil until the sugar is caramelized and light brown. Place each ramekin on a small dessert plate and serve immediately.

Wine pairing The classic pairing for this creamy dessert is a mature Sauternes, which mimics the dessert's rich caramel flavors. Interesting alternatives from lesser-known regions of France that also use a similar blend of Sauvignon Blanc/Sémillon grapes come from Loupiac and Ste.-Croix-du-Mont, which lie just across the river from Sauternes.

Old-Fashioned Caramel Apple Buckle

BILL CARDWELL

Apple picking is a popular fall tradition in St. Louis. In homage to this pastime, Bill Cardwell offers an apple buckle, which is a simple cake with fruit added to the batter. The streusel-like topping "buckles" once the dessert is baked. Top with vanilla bean ice cream to make it all-American.

SERVES 6

1 tablespoon butter

8 medium Granny Smith apples, peeled, cored, and sliced into thin wedges

2 tablespoons turbinado sugar

¼ teaspoon ground cinnamon

Pinch of sea salt

2 tablespoons Calvados or apple brandy

2 tablespoons heavy cream

½ cup golden raisins

1 cup granulated sugar

1 cup all-purpose flour

1 teaspoon baking powder

1 large egg, lightly beaten

4 tablespoons (½ stick) unsalted butter, melted

Preheat the oven to 325°F. In a large skillet over medium-low heat, melt the butter. Add half of the apples in a single layer, and allow them to brown on the undersides, 1 to 2 minutes. Sprinkle with 1 tablespoon of the turbinado sugar, and allow it to melt and caramelize. Transfer to a platter and repeat with the remaining apples and turbinado sugar.

Return all of the cooked apples to the skillet. Add the cinnamon, salt, and Calvados. Using a long match, carefully light the Calvados and allow the flames to burn off. Add the cream and simmer, stirring occasionally, until the mixture is thickened and the apples are glazed.

Remove the apple mixture from the heat and stir in the raisins. Transfer to a 9-inch-square baking dish or other baking dish that allows the filling to be about 1½ inches deep.

In a medium bowl, whisk together the sugar, flour, and baking powder. Add the egg and use 2 forks to blend it in. Using the forks, slowly mix in 3 tablespoons of the melted butter until the mixture has pea-size lumps and resembles wet sand.

Sprinkle the topping lightly over the apples to cover the fruit; do not pack or pat down the topping. Drizzle the remaining 1 tablespoon of melted butter over the topping. Bake approximately 15 minutes, until golden brown. Serve warm.

Wine pairing To accent the apple flavors, serve this fall dessert with a German or Austrian late-harvest Riesling at the ripeness level of Beerenauslese. Or, if you want to echo the sweetness of the raisins, enjoy this with a tawny port.

Old-Fashioned Strawberry Shortcake

LARRY FORGIONE

No one has done more to keep traditional American cooking alive than Larry Forgione. His shortcake batter features hard-cooked eggs, a classic old-fashioned addition; egg yolks were used this way in the late 1800s to add moisture and give the shortcakes a creamy texture. This was James Beard's mother's recipe, and James passed it on to Larry. I can't imagine making shortcake any other way.

SERVES 6

2 cups all-purpose flour

¼ cup granulated sugar

2 mashed hard-cooked egg yolks

1 tablespoon plus ½ teaspoon baking powder

6 tablespoons cold unsalted butter, cut into
   small pieces

¾ cup heavy cream

2 tablespoons unsalted butter, melted

2 tablespoons turbinado sugar

½ cup strawberry jam

1 tablespoon black sesame seeds

3 pints fresh strawberries, washed, hulled,
   and halved

2 tablespoons granulated sugar

1 cup heavy cream

2 tablespoons confectioners' sugar

1 teaspoon vanilla extract

MAKE THE SHORTCAKES: Preheat the oven to 350°F. Combine the flour, sugar, mashed egg yolks, and baking powder in a bowl. Cut in the cold butter with a fork or a pastry blender. Add the cream, mixing until the dough just comes together. Do not overwork or the shortcakes will become tough. Gather the dough, making a flattened round, and wrap it in plastic wrap. Refrigerate for 30 minutes to relax the dough.

Remove the dough from the refrigerator. Lightly flour a work surface. Using a rolling pin, roll the dough to a thickness of ½ inch. Cut into 6 rounds with a 2-inch floured biscuit cutter. Place the shortcakes on a greased baking sheet, brush the shortcakes with the melted butter, and top with the turbinado sugar.

Bake the shortcakes until golden brown, about 16 minutes. Transfer to a wire rack and allow to cool to room temperature.

Mix the strawberry jam with the black sesame seeds. Set aside.

Mix the strawberries with the granulated sugar and allow them to macerate until ready to serve. Meanwhile, in the bowl of an electric mixer, make the whipped cream by combining the cream, confectioners' sugar, and vanilla.

To assemble the shortcakes, use a brush to paint the strawberry jam on each plate in one straight line. Cut each shortcake in half and place the bottom half of each on the jam line. Heap some of the macerated strawberries on top of the shortcake halves, then spoon the whipped cream on top of the strawberries. Place the top half of the shortcake on top and serve immediately.

Wine pairing The quaint region of Niagara-on-the-Lake in Ontario, Canada, produces some of the world's most amazing Icewines made with Riesling and Vidal Blanc grapes, either of which would be sensational with this strawberry dessert.

Oozing Flourless Chocolate Cakes

GALE GAND

Oozing. Molten. Gooey. However you describe this modern classic dessert, it's always a crowd-pleaser. Best of all, the cakes can be prepared ahead, refrigerated, and baked at the last minute.

SERVES 6

½ pound semisweet chocolate

½ cup (1 stick) unsalted butter, plus additional
    for buttering ramekins

3 large eggs

½ cup heavy cream

1 teaspoon brown sugar

Confectioners' sugar, for garnish

Preheat the oven to 425°F. Butter six 4-ounce ramekins or ovenproof dessert cups. Place a saucepan of water on the stove to simmer.

In a heatproof bowl, combine the chocolate and butter and place them over the saucepan of simmering water, making sure the water doesn't touch the bowl. When the butter and chocolate are melted, remove from the heat and let cool, stirring occasionally, for about 5 minutes.

Crack the eggs into the bowl of a standing mixer with a whisk attachment, and place the bowl briefly over the simmering water, stirring constantly until the eggs are warm to the touch. Whisk the eggs with the mixer until they are light yellow and very fluffy.

Fold the chocolate mixture into the whipped eggs until no streaks show. The batter will deflate. Fill the prepared ramekins three-quarters full. You can make the cakes up to this point, then refrigerate them until you are ready to bake. If you bake them when they are still cold, add 5 minutes to the baking time, or let them come to room temperature before baking. Bake for 10 to 14 minutes, depending on how liquid you like the centers.

In the bowl of an electric mixer fitted with a whisk attachment, combine the cream and brown sugar. Whisk until stiff peaks form.

To serve, turn the cakes out onto dessert plates. Sprinkle with confectioners' sugar, top with a dollop of sweetened whipped cream, and serve immediately.

Wine pairing Recioto della Valpolicella wines from Italy's Veneto region are full-bodied dessert wines made from dried grapes. Such a concentrated, semisweet wine is a fitting complement to the warm chocolate flavors of these cakes.

Three-Pear Cake
(Gâteau aux Trois Poires)

PATRICIA WELLS

Patricia Wells's recipes reflect her long-term love affair with France. The three pears mentioned in the title refer to the varieties that she used to grow in her garden in Provence, but only one type is used in this recipe. She shares: "This is a variation on my popular Apple Lady's Apple Cake. I have fiddled with it quite a bit, substituting yogurt for milk (which gives a moister texture to the cake), highlighting the pear flavor with a touch of pear *eau de vie*, and boosting the acidity with a touch of lemon. I serve this with either buttermilk sorbet or pear sorbet."

SERVES 8

Unsalted butter, for buttering pan

½ cup all-purpose flour, plus additional for
    dusting pan

⅓ cup sugar

1 tablespoon baking powder

⅛ teaspoon fine sea salt

½ teaspoon vanilla extract

2 large eggs, lightly beaten

1 tablespoon vegetable oil

1 tablespoon pear *eau de vie* or pear brandy

⅓ cup plain yogurt

Finely grated zest of 1 lemon

4 large pears (about 2 pounds), peeled, cored,
    and cut lengthwise into sixteenths

⅓ cup sugar

1 large egg, lightly beaten

1 tablespoon pear *eau de vie* or pear brandy

Finely grated zest of 1 lemon

Preheat the oven to 425°F. Butter a 9-inch springform pan and dust with flour; set aside.

Combine the flour, sugar, baking powder, and salt in a large bowl and stir to blend. Add the vanilla, eggs, oil, *eau de vie*, yogurt, and lemon zest, and stir until well blended. Add the pears and stir gently to thoroughly coat the fruit with the batter.

Spoon the mixture into the prepared cake pan. Place the pan in the center of the oven and bake until fairly firm and golden, about 40 minutes.

In a small bowl, combine the sugar, egg, eau de vie, and lemon zest, and stir to blend. Set aside.

Once the cake is firm and golden, remove the cake from the oven and pour the sugar mixture on top of the cake, evening out with a spatula. Return the cake to the oven and bake until the top is a deep golden brown and the cake feels quite firm when pressed with a fingertip, about 10 minutes more, for a total baking time of 50 minutes.

Transfer to a wire rack to cool. After 10 minutes, run a knife along the inside of the pan. Release and remove the sides of the springform pan, leaving the cake on the pan base. Serve at room temperature, cutting into thin wedges.

Wine pairing *Complement the hint of brandy in this favorite cake of Patricia Wells by pouring an Australian "sticky," a Sauternes, or a late-harvest Riesling.*

Contributing Chefs

MICHAEL ANTHONY was appointed executive chef of Gramercy Tavern in New York City in September 2006. Under his leadership, the restaurant was awarded its second three-star review from *The New York Times*. He was formerly the executive chef of Blue Hill at Stone Barns, the co-executive chef of Blue Hill in Manhattan, and the *chef de cuisine* at March.

DAPHNE ARAUJO lives with her husband, Bart, in Calistoga, California, where they own and operate Araujo Wine Estates. In addition to making exquisite wines, the Araujos produce olive oil and honey.

DAN BARBER is executive chef and co-owner of Blue Hill in New York City and Blue Hill at Stone Barns in Pocantico Hills, New York, both of which received three-star reviews from the *New York Times*. In 2006, Dan was named Best Chef: New York City by the James Beard Foundation.

LIDIA MATTICCHIO BASTIANICH, host of the 39-part public television show *Lidia's Italian Table*, is regarded as the "First Lady" of Italian cuisine in the United States. In New York, Lidia is owner of the award-winning Felidia restaurant and with her son, Joseph, runs Becco. A born teacher and educator, Lidia is also the author of *Lidia's Italian Table, Lidia's Italian-American Kitchen*, and other widely regarded cookbooks.

CHRISTOPHER BENNETT, chef and co-owner of Melrose Bar & Grill, went into the restaurant business following a six-year career as a research engineer in the microelectronics industry. In 1990, Bennett and his wife, Julie, opened the first Doug Arango's in Palm Desert, California, then moved the restaurant to Hollywood, which in September 2007 became Melrose Bar & Grill in the same location.

VINCENT P. BOMMARITO, a graduate of the Culinary Institute of America, has worked in kitchens across the country. In 1990, he was named Chef of the Year by Chefs of America. Vincent has served as president and executive chef of Tony's Restaurant in St. Louis since 1993. For more than 40 years, Tony's has been renowned as featuring the finest food, unparalleled service, and a distinctive, elegant ambience.

DANIEL BOULUD is the chef-owner of five award-winning restaurants, as well as Feast & Fêtes catering. He is also the author of six cookbooks and the creator of Connoisseur gourmet products. While he hails from Lyon, France, it is in New York that he has truly made his mark on the culinary scene. Boulud's many culinary accolades include the James Beard Foundation awards for Outstanding Restaurateur, Best Chef: New York City, and Outstanding Chef of the Year. His restaurant, Daniel, has been named "one of the ten best restaurants in the world" by the *International Herald Tribune* and has earned a four-star rating from the *New York Times.*

BERTRAND BOUQUIN joined the Broadmoor as executive chef of the Summit Restaurant in January 2005, after his role as executive chef at the Maisonette in Cincinnati, Ohio, the longest holder of the Mobil Five-Star restaurant award. Bouquin trained under world-famous chefs Alain Ducasse, Daniel Boulud, and Jean-Pierre Bruneau. Bouquin has worked at some of the best restaurants in the United States, including Club XIX at the Lodge at Pebble Beach, and Restaurant Daniel and Café Boulud in New York City, and has held key positions at several Michelin-starred restaurants in Europe.

TERRANCE BRENNAN is chef-proprietor of two highly acclaimed New York restaurants and the man behind Artisanal Premium Cheese. Following positions at several Washington, D.C., restaurants, Terrance cooked at Le Cirque and worked in many of Europe's greatest kitchens, including Taillevent, Le Tour d'Argent, Gualtiero Marchesi, La Gavroche, and Le Moulin de Mougins. In 1993, Terrance opened his first restaurant, Picholine, which earned its first of two three-star reviews from the *New York Times,* and introduced the traditional European cheese course to American fine dining. In 2001, he opened Artisanal, a bistro, fromagerie, and wine bar. In 2003 Terrance launched Artisanal Premium Cheese, dedicated to the selection, maturation, and distribution of the world's finest artisanal cheeses. He is the author of *Artisanal Cooking: A Chef Shares His Passion for Handcrafting Great Meals at Home.*

SCOTT BRYAN began his career at Bob Kinkead's Harvest Restaurant in Boston and at 21 Federal on Nantucket. He worked in such illustrious kitchens as Gotham Bar & Grill, Restaurant Bouley, Le Bernardin, and Lespinasse in New York City and Square One in San Francisco. In 1994, Scott was named executive chef at Soleil, and then moved to Alison on Dominick Street, Luma, and then Indigo. Scott Bryan was most recently a partner and chef at Veritas, which is known for pairing food with its 100,000-bottle wine list.

BILL CARDWELL graduated from the Culinary Institute of America and apprenticed under Chef Albert Stockli at the Four Seasons restaurant in New York City. Cardwell's at the Plaza, in St. Louis, is continuously ranked as one of the Midwest's top restaurants. Bill is a founding member of the Saint Louis Originals, a group dedicated to celebrating the spirit, strength, and unique experiences offered by independently owned restaurants, whose chefs and owners live, work, play, and invest in their communities.

BRYAN CARR learned professional cooking from French chefs in California and from decades-long study of culinary traditions. Bryan lives with his wife, Diane, and their daughter, Olivia, in Clayton, Missouri, where they operate Pomme Restaurant and Pomme Café & Wine Bar.

NARSAI DAVID is the food and wine editor at KCBS in San Francisco. For sixteen years he owned Narsai's, the renowned restaurant in Kensington, California, with a wine list described by the *New York Times* as "one of the ten finest in the world." A former columnist for the *San Francisco Chronicle* and the *San Francisco Examiner,* Narsai added "winemaker" to his résumé in 2000 with the release of his Narsai Cabernet Sauvignon from the Narsai and Venus David Vineyards in St. Helena.

BERNARD DERVIEUX started his career at age thirteen as an apprentice charcutier in Vienne, France. He worked with Paul Bocuse in Lyon and Roger Vergé at Le Moulin de Mougins. Paul Bocuse sent Bernard to the United States to work at Le Français, in Wheeling, Illinois, as a saucier/sous chef under the supervision of Jean Banchet. He then worked at the Pump Room in Chicago, the Beverly Hills Hotel in Los Angeles, and the Grand Champions Resort in Indian Wells, California. In 1987, Bernard opened the highly regarded Cuistot near Palm Springs.

JAMES FIALA, a native St. Louisian, attended culinary school in San Francisco and apprenticed with Jeremiah Tower, Paul Bartolotta, and Daniel Boulud. Today Jimmy owns and operates three unique restaurants in the St. Louis area—Acero, The Crossing, and Liluma.

LARRY FORGIONE has had a long and distinguished career as one of America's most respected chefs. As chef-proprietor of An American Place (New York, St. Louis), he has been the recipient of numerous awards, including Chef of the Year from both the James Beard Foundation and the Culinary Institute of America. Larry was chosen "as the pioneer and catalyst of New American Cuisine" in *Life* magazine's feature "The 50 Most Influential Americans of the Baby Boom Generation." He is the author of the award-winning *An American Place Cookbook* and co-founder of American Spoon Foods in Petoskey, Michigan.

JOSHUA GALLIANO grew up in south Louisiana. After receiving a master's degree in political science from Louisiana State University, he earned a Grand Diplôme from Le Cordon Bleu in London and worked at restaurants Roussillon and Angela Hartnett's Menu at the Connaught Hotel. Josh returned to New Orleans and cooked with Tory McPhail at Commander's Palace, for Daniel Boulud at his eponymous restaurant, and in St. Louis at An American Place with Larry Forgione.

GALE GAND was schooled at La Varenne in Paris before opening Trio, Brasserie T, and then later the renowned four-star Mobil, five-diamond AAA, Relais & Chateaux Relais Gourmand restaurant Tru with culinary partner Rick Tramonto. She is an accomplished cookbook author with six titles to her credit, including her most recent, *Chocolate and Vanilla*.

ALEXANDRA GUARNASCHELLI graduated from Barnard College in 1991, then decided to explore her culinary interests and began working under the tutelage of Larry Forgione. Guarnaschelli moved to France to study at La Varenne and then began a *stage* at the Michelin three-star restaurant Guy Savoy. She was promoted to sous chef at La Butte Chaillot, another Savoy establishment. After seven years in France, Guarnaschelli joined the venerable Daniel Boulud at Restaurant Daniel, and then headed west to Los Angeles to join Joachim Splichal's Patina. In 2003, Guarnaschelli became executive chef at Butter in New York. She is also a chef-instructor at New York City's Institute of Culinary Education.

THOMAS KELLER began his culinary career at a young age, working at the Palm Beach restaurant managed by his mother. After serving apprenticeships throughout the United States, Keller relocated to France in 1983, where he worked in several Michelin-starred restaurants, including Guy Savoy and Taillevent. He later returned to New York, where he gained renown at La Reserve and Restaurant Raphael. In 1994, he opened the highly praised French Laundry in Yountville, California, followed by the bistro Bouchon in 1998. In 2004, Keller opened Per Se in New York. He now has eight restaurants. Keller is the author of two cookbooks, *The French Laundry* and *Bouchon*. He has collected many accolades within the past decade, including America's Best Chef from *Time* magazine and consecutive Best Chef awards from the James Beard Foundation. Most recently, he was recognized as Chef of the Year by the Culinary Institute of America.

SIRIO MACCIONI has dedicated his life to the restaurant business. Born in Montecatini Terme, Italy, he trained in Paris and Hamburg and held apprenticeships in Italy and France. After moving to New York, he developed loyal followings at Delmonico's and the Colony restaurant. In 1974, he opened Le Cirque in the Mayfair with his wife, Egidiana, and their three sons, Mario, Marco, and Mauro. It became and remains one of New York's most beloved restaurants. In 1997, under the new name of Le Cirque 2000, the restaurant moved into the New York Palace Hotel; in 2006 the Maccionis reopened their long-standing restaurant under its original name, Le Cirque. Among the many awards it has won are the coveted James Beard Foundation Restaurant of the Year award and (for Le Cirque 2000) the Wine Spectator's Grand Award. The Maccionis have been designated living landmarks by the New York Landmarks Conservancy. In 2004, to much acclaim, Maccioni released his autobiography, *Sirio: The Story of My Life and Le Cirque.*

CHRISTOPHER MANNING attended classes at the Le Cordon Bleu cooking schools in Paris, London, and Florence before enrolling at San Francisco's prestigious California Culinary Academy. He earned a professional degree there in 2000 and worked under acclaimed chef Laurent Manrique at the Campton Place Restaurant. In 2001, Chris joined Étoile at Domaine Chandon.

MATTHEW MCGUIRE was the owner and operator of King Louie's restaurant in St. Louis from 1994 until 2007. During that time, King Louie's gained acclaim both regionally and nationally for being a cutting-edge culinary destination. Matthew received his BFA in painting and art history from the Art Institute of Chicago.

KEVIN NASHAN was born and raised in Santa Fe, New Mexico, where he grew up working in the family-owned restaurant, La Tertulia, which was in business for 27 years. After graduating from St. Louis University, he attended the Culinary Institute of America in Hyde Park, New York. With plans to eventually return to St. Louis, he spent five years traveling and working in restaurants around the world, including Le Français, Commander's Palace, Daniel, and Martin Berasategui. He has been the chef-owner of Sidney Street Cafe in St. Louis since 2003.

CINDY PAWLCYN earned her degree in hospitality and tourism management from the University of Wisconsin. She moved to the Napa Valley in 1983 and opened Mustards Grill, her first of more than a dozen restaurants. She has written three cookbooks (*Fog City Diner Cookbook, Mustards Grill Cookbook,* and *Big Small Plates*) and has been nominated twice for a James Beard Foundation award for Best Chef: California. Cindy is now co-owner of Mustards Grill, Cindy's Backstreet Kitchen, and Go Fish in California's Napa Valley.

RICHARD PERRY's taste for hearty, fresh food dates back to his childhood on an Illinois farm. He has had a distinguished career in the culinary arts, both as a chef and as a writer. His most notable restaurant, the Jefferson Avenue Boarding House, received recognition from *Cook's* magazine and *Esquire,* and awards from *Travel/Holiday* and the *Mobile Guide.* He devotes much of his time to promoting gastronomic education through the Society for American Cuisine, of which he is the founder, and the Chaîne des Rôtisseurs.

NORA POUILLON is a native of Austria and an internationally renowned chef and owner of Restaurant Nora and Asia Nora in Washington, D.C. Opened in 1979, Restaurant Nora became the nation's first certified organic restaurant in 1999. Nora is an ardent supporter of small farms and initiated the Fresh Farm Markets, producer-only farmers' markets in the Washington, D.C., area. Widely recognized for her pioneering work, Nora is a founding member of the Chefs Collaborative and a board member of Women Chefs and Restaurateurs.

RICHARD REDDINGTON did not begin his culinary career until after graduating from Miami University of Ohio with a degree in business. Realizing that he wanted to cook, he started working at San Francisco's La Folie and Postrio, then went to Park Avenue Cafe in New York City. He sojourned at L'Arpege and Le Moulin de Mougins in France, and then at Restaurant Daniel in New York. Richard returned to California and cooked at Spago Beverly Hills, Chapeau, and Jardinière. In 2000, he began a four-year tenure as executive chef at Auberge du Soleil in the Napa Valley and then cooked at San Francisco's Masa before recently taking the leap and opening Redd's in Yountville.

JULIE RIDLON is caterer/owner of Chanterelle Catering and co-founder of Clayton Farmer's Market. Her current projects include Chair of the Missouri Chef's Collaborative of the St. Louis Culinary Society and development of an inner-city after-school culinary program to encourage potential young chefs.

ERIC RIPERT is grateful for his early exposure to two cuisines—he was born in Antibes, France, then moved as a young child to Andorra, just inside the Spanish border. His family instilled their own passion for food in the young Ripert, and at the age of fifteen he left home to attend culinary school in Perpignan. Later Eric honed his culinary skills working under Joël Robuchon in Paris and with Jean-Louis Palladin in Washington, D.C. Since 1991 he has been with Le Bernardin, and in 1995 he took over the kitchen after the untimely death of his predecessor, Gilbert Le Coze. Since then, he has led Le Bernardin to consistently top ratings from the *New York Times* (four stars), the Michelin Guide (three stars), and the Zagat guide. Ripert has published two cookbooks, *A Return to Cooking* with Michael Ruhlman and *Le Bernardin Cookbook* with Maguy Le Coze.

LOU ROOK III has had a passion for food since he was a teenager working at his family's diner. A graduate of the University of Missouri and the Culinary Institute of America, Lou began his culinary career at the Trellis Restaurant in Williamsburg, Virginia. He then returned to the Midwest and served as chef in various St. Louis restaurants before becoming executive chef at Annie Gunn's in the Chesterfield Valley. Under his leadership, Annie Gunn's has received numerous accolades, including the "Top Tables" selection in *Gourmet* and many awards of excellence from *Wine Spectator*. Chef Rook is an active member of the James Beard Foundation and donates his culinary gifts to many charity events in St. Louis and throughout Missouri.

MICHAEL ROZZI worked at many prominent restaurants in the Hamptons on Long Island, including the Fish Net, the Falcon, Le Chef, the Inn at Quogue, and Crazy Dog, before assuming his position as executive chef of Della Femina in 1996.

PILAR SANCHEZ is the chef-owner of Pilar in St. Helena, California. She majored in biology at Santa Barbara City College before moving on to a pastry major at UCLA's Extension School. She received her degree in hotel and restaurant management and culinary arts from Oxnard College. Following stints at Santa Barbara's Four Seasons Biltmore, Ernie's, and the Four Seasons Clift in San Francisco, Pilar and husband, Didier Lenders, opened Café del Sol in Paris. Pilar spent five years at the Relais & Chateaux Meadowood Napa Valley resort as *chef de cuisine* and banquet chef, and then at the Culinary Institute of America as executive chef of the Wine Spectator restaurant.

CELINA TIO's culinary career began when she was eight years old, cooking and baking for family and friends. After receiving a degree from Drexel University in Hotel and Restaurant Management, she contemplated going to culinary school but opted for the hands-on experience of working her way up at the Ritz-Carlton Hotel. From there, Chef Tio spent five years with Walt Disney World in Orlando, Florida, opening three of their specialty restaurants, the last two years spent as the chef of Narcoossee's at the Grand Floridian Resort. Having been at the American six years, she has already garnered many accolades, both locally and nationally. She was chosen as the 2005 chef of the year by *Chef* magazine and was most recently named the James Beard Foundation's 2007 Best Chef: Midwest.

RICK TRAMONTO became a legend on the Chicago food scene with his most famous restaurant, Tru. As culinary director and executive chef of Cenitare Restaurants LLC, Chef Tramonto has four Chicago restaurants, including Tru, Tramonto's Steak & Seafood, Osteria de Tramonto, and the RT Sushi Bar & Lounge. In 1994, *Food & Wine* recognized Tramonto as one of the Top Ten Best New Chefs in the country, and in 1995 he was recognized as one of America's Rising Star Chefs by Robert Mondavi. Under his vision, Tru became a four-star Mobil, five-diamond AAA restaurant, and garnered the coveted Relais-Gourmand property by Relais & Chateaux. Chef Tramonto has received many honors from the James Beard Foundation Awards including Best Chef: Midwest Region (2002), nominations for Best New Restaurant (2000), and three consecutive nominations for Outstanding Service (Tru), as well as Grand Award status from *Wine*

Spectator Magazine. He is also an accomplished cookbook author, including *Amuse-Bouche, Tru: A Cookbook from the Legendary Chicago Restaurant*, and *Fantastico!*

CHARLIE TROTTER has become a culinary superstar through his eponymous Charlie Trotter's, regarded as one of the finest restaurants in the world. It has received five stars from the Mobil Travel Guide, five diamonds from AAA, and ten James Beard Foundation awards, including Outstanding Restaurant (2000) and Outstanding Chef (1999). *Wine Spectator* named it The Best Restaurant in the World for Wine & Food in 1998 and America's Best Restaurant in 2000. Chef Trotter is the author of fourteen cookbooks and two management books, and is the host of the nationally aired, award-winning PBS cooking series *The Kitchen Sessions with Charlie Trotter*. He also produces a line of organic and gourmet products. Beyond his numerous culinary accolades, Chef Trotter devotes much of his time to philanthropic activities, especially the Charlie Trotter Culinary Education Foundation, which supports careers in the culinary arts. In 2005, Chef Trotter was awarded the Humanitarian of the Year award by the International Association of Culinary Professionals for his service to the community.

JEAN-GEORGES VONGERICHTEN is one of the world's most famous chefs. He oversees a constellation of three- and four-star restaurants in the United States, United Kingdom, Shanghai, and Hong Kong. Born and raised on the outskirts of Strasbourg in Alsace, France, Jean-Georges trained as an apprentice to Chef Paul Haeberlin, later working with Paul Bocuse and master-chef Louis Outhier at L'Oasis in the south of France. While working and traveling to Asia, Jean-Georges developed his love for the exotic and aromatic flavors of the East. He has won a host of awards during his distinguished career, including awards from the James Beard Foundation for Best New Restaurant (Vong), Outstanding Chef, and Who's Who of Food and Beverage and Best Cookbook award for *Asian Flavors of Jean-Georges*. His restaurant Jean

Georges earned a rare four-star rating from the *New York Times*. He has published several cookbooks, including *Simple Cuisine, Cooking at Home with a Four Star Chef*, and *Simple to Spectacular*. Jean-Georges is Master Cook for *Food & Wine* magazine and has appeared on *Live! with Regis and Kelly*, the *Today Show, Good Morning America, Martha Stewart Living, TV Food Network*, and in the 1995 PBS series *In Julia's Kitchen with Master Chefs*.

DAVID WALTUCK first began cooking while attending City College of New York. After graduating Phi Beta Kappa with a degree in biological oceanography, he briefly attended the Culinary Institute of America and spent two years as lunch chef at La Petite Ferme in New York City. David opened Chanterelle at the age of twenty-four with his wife, Karen, in a then-remote section of SoHo. David's first book, *Staff Meals from Chanterelle,* was published in July of 2000, and a second book is slated for fall 2008. Among the many accolades for David and Chanterelle are Best Chef: New York City from the James Beard Foundation in 2007 and for Outstanding Restaurant from the James Beard Foundation in 2004.

PATRICIA WELLS, journalist, author, and cooking teacher, is an American who has lived in Paris since 1980. She is the author of ten books, including *Bistro Cooking, Simply French, The Provence Cookbook*, and *Vegetable Harvest*. She is the only woman and the only foreigner to serve as restaurant critic of the French newsweekly *L'Express*. Since 1980 she has been the food critic for the *International Herald Tribune*. She is the recipient of numerous awards, including the Chevalier de l'Ordre des Arts et des Lettres, for her contributions to French culture. She has received an honorary degree in gastronomic journalism from the University of Wisconsin-Milwaukee.

AARON WRIGHT started his culinary career in Seattle bistros. He opened Andaluca in the Mayflower Park Hotel and was quickly promoted to sous chef. He later opened Earth & Ocean in the W Hotel. Aaron was hired by Canlis Restaurant in 2000 and has been its executive chef since 2002.

Sources

Cabernet Wine Vinegar
www.napavalleyproducts.com

Chestnut Purée and Marron Glacé
www.markys.com
(800) 522-8427

Foie Gras
www.dartagnan.com
(800) 327-8246
www.hudsonvalleyfoiegras.com
(845) 292-2500

Hazelnut Flour
www.kingarthurflour.com
(800) 827-6836
www.bobsredmill.com
(800) 553-2258

Huckleberries
www.oregonmushrooms.com
(800) 682-0036

Oils and Vinegars
www.cybercucina.com
(800) 796-0116
www.epicurepantry.com
www.lepicerie.com
(866) 350-7575

Venison
www.cervena.com
(800) 877-1187
www.chicagogame.us
(888) 456-5656
www.dartagnan.com
(800) 327-8246
www.shafferfarms.com
(800) 446-3745

Wild Mushrooms, Truffles, and Truffle Oil
www.dartagnan.com
(800) 327-8246
www.earthy.com (Earthy Delights)
(800) 367-4709

Index